THE PHYSIO

By the same author

fiction
Wilfred and Eileen
The English Lover
In Flight
Come Back
Summer in February
Night Windows
The Churchill Secret

non-fiction
Good Enough? (with Chris Cowdrey)
The Learning Game
The Following Game
Being Betjeman(n)

THE PHYSIO

JONATHAN SMITH

Foreword by
Ed Smith

G

Cambridge, UK

Galileo Publishers
16 Woodlands Road, Great Shelford,
Cambridge
CB22 5LW UK
www.galileopublishing.co.uk

Distributed in the USA by SCB Distributors
15608 S. New Century Drive Gardena,
CA 90248-2129, USA

Australia: Peribo Pty Limited
58 Beaumont Road
Mount Kuring-Gai, NSW 2080
Australia

ISBN 978-1915530-554

Printed in the EU

You got me singing ...
... that I'd like to carry on
Leonard Cohen

Everybody's got a hungry heart
Bruce Springsteen

For Jane Cast, physiotherapist

FOREWORD by Ed Smith

One of the many qualities I admire in my father is his hesitancy. And I hesitate now, before writing this foreword to his new book, *The Physio*. I've never written about Dad's work in this way, or his life for that matter, and I'm daunted. I'm also, as we'd say in professional sport, 'over-matched' in this company. Because Dad is so good at writing concisely and personally, with disarming lightness and yet acute perceptiveness. And that's exactly what a good foreword might do, which makes me conscious of all the ways I can fall short.

The Physio begins with an author writing his own name in pencil, trying to reverse – or hold at bay – micrographia, one of the early symptoms of Parkinson's, a condition which Dad has had for a number of years. He is having to relearn how to write – that is, relearning how to scratch the pencil onto the paper, not relearning how to order and shape sentences. But the outward and inner journey are conjoined. Physically, he is writing down his name to nurture his body and his health. Metaphorically, he is affirming who he is – still creating, still a writer. So the reader shares in a kind of rebirth, even though Dad would probably howl in horror at such a Californian-sounding concept.

As usual with Dad, he didn't tell anyone he was writing another book, aged 82. He just did it. My first reaction was to think of the physical triumph: 50,000 words typed, and none typed easily. That the words would be good ones was never in doubt; that they emerged at all is a serious achievement.

The Physio sets up a distinction between two kinds of life – one significantly given over to books (his own life) and the second mostly devoted to bodies, especially fixing bodies (his physiotherapist's life). The book alternates and contrasts these two modes or spheres – bookishness and physicality – while ultimately uniting or reconciling them. In gaining more mastery of his body, Dad is able to write another book. So the structure is multi-layered: his physio is simultaneously the subject and the catalyst of the object that you're now holding in your hand. Hence the short section in *The Physio* about the centrality of a book's feel, touch and smell is not incidental. It's a nod to the book's (this book's) central theme: the relationship between ideas and materiality.

Dad has always disliked the concept of genres, so I won't attempt to describe this one – beyond saying it's his own genre. He's telling a story about someone else, he's telling a story about himself, and he's also telling a story about story-telling – how it happens, and what makes it exciting.

Because where Dad's novels and radio plays are often anchored in facts, his non-fiction books are also partly about fiction. I do not mean that he invents facts, but instead that his non-fiction is full of hints and explorations about what drew him towards the subjects of other work. However subtly, writers are always writing about their own work.

These are some of my favourite passages of *The Physio*, partly for the personal reason that it takes me back to research trips we took as a family. Visiting the Hôtel Biron in Paris when Dad was writing a play about Rodin; his fascination with the intense (and ultimately deeply sad) friendship between Robert Louis Stevenson and W.E.Henley, which led to his play *Silver*; the backstory of his first novel, *Wilfred and Eileen*, which was 'given' to him by a student in one of his English lessons, who knew about a family manuscript relating to a remarkable First World War love story. (The student was the future historian, Sir Anthony Seldon.)

A writer's opening subject is often revealing, and the first page of *Wilfred and Eileen* (1976) explores a theme that runs through much of Dad's fiction and non-fiction: types of intelligence, especially his own ambiguous dissatisfaction with highly academic intelligence. On the eve of a Cambridge May Ball, the protagonist, Wilfred Willett, is tiring of a place 'too full of clever men' (though he was glad to be one of them):

> One could be articulate to the point of lunacy and Wilfred sometimes feared his friends would arrive at that as they qualified, organised escape clauses and strove – always on guard and light of foot – to be absolutely, scintillatingly accurate in every nuance of perception.

The author firmly lines up with Wilfred's impatience with over-intellectualising. Dad is entirely convinced he's not an intellectual while obviously being one. I don't think this is false modesty – as with some clever people, who, when they say they aren't particularly adept at 'thinking' are actually asking you to disagree with the assessment – but instead it is a question of priorities. I think he has a genuine concern – a writer's concern – that ideas can get in the way when they are too close to the surface. It's as though he feels that to be creative – as a novelist seeks to be creative – you must be wary about ideas as well as open to them. Ideas might be on tap, but ideas shouldn't be on top.

Here, fifty years on in *The Physio*, Dad returns to the theme. He describes "an elusive, tricky, equivocal writer. He's clever but he plays don't-let's-be-too-clever, which is a very English thing; he was an intellectual who claimed not to be able to think; a suburban who loathed suburbia."

Dad's subject is E.M.Forster, though much of it applies to himself. And in many ways, Dad's mixture of sensitivity and anti-intellectual intelligence as a writer (and hesitancy, to borrow Forster's term) makes him very Forsterian.

But there is one very significant difference, which is also bound up with the creation of *The Physio*. Dad has a deep love of sport – perhaps equal to his love of books – and his interest in sport is powered by a fascination and admiration for physical virtuosity. With the greatest respect to Forster, it's hard to imagine him being a decent fullback in a rugby-crazed Welsh school 1st XV – which Dad was, in Brecon in 1959. Dad would interrupt immediately to say he wasn't naturally very good. But if he made himself good at rugby because that's what everyone around him respected, then that's even more revealing.

He rates winners and doers, too, with a little more sneaking regard than a sensitive novelist likes to admit to. And that deep interest in physical 'alpha' underpins his reverence for his physio. Whereas he is always re-arranging his favourite books in his writer's hut, she is skipping up Mont Blanc. Askance respect for putting physicality more at the heart of life is a central theme of the book – and Dad's whole sensibility.

As a kid, when we were driving to places he was researching for a novel, or just back to Wales for walking holidays, I'd watch his hands on the steering wheel. (We give ourselves away with our hands, don't we?) Slight, delicate, gentle – a writer's hands. But also sun-flecked and tanned, like a 1960s American golfer – the hands of someone who's outside a lot, almost a countryman. Two sides of life, two sides of a life. Both groups imagined him as one of their own; neither side was quite right.

Navigating the tension between the two has sustained his curiosity and creativity – never more so than in *The Physio*.

PART ONE

Every morning, without fail, I practise writing my name. I
always tear off a fresh sheet of ruled paper – it has to be
a fresh sheet, and it has to be paper of the finest quality – and,
taking my time, with my left hand I very deliberately set about
forming the letters J-o-n-a and so on. It's a bit like being back
in primary school. It's a bit like being back in the late 1940s,
sitting at my little wooden desk chanting my tables and writing
the alphabet with my teacher, Miss Evans, standing there at the
front of the class, a small upright lady with a perm.

'Come on, children, pencils ready,' Miss Evans would say in
her Welsh chapel voice, 'and let's do our A B C, shall we, nice
and big, children. A is for apple, B is for ball, and for bat, yes,
thank you, that's quite right, Jonathan Smith, but put your hand
up if you want to speak, there's a good boy, and C is for cat. Use
all the space between the lines, children, swoop up, don't be tiny,
we don't want tiny, keep your pencils on the paper as you go
and swoop up, up, and loop down, fill the lines, nice and big, so
each letter is sitting on the line, like birds on a wire, and what
does that spell?'

It spells

J-o-n-a-t-h-a-n

I'm learning to write all over again. My micrographia was
one of the symptoms, an early sign that all was not well.

Right
Ready?
Three deep breaths

In through the nose
Hold it
And
Out through the mouth
In through the nose
Hold it
And
Out through the mouth

And I'm also learning, if it's not too late, how to breathe.

-Jonathan.
-Yes?
-You're not with me.
-I am.
-You're not. You switched off. You were gone. If this is to be any help you've got to keep at it.
-I'm with you now.
-Right, I was saying, try and get your glutes, your bottom muscles to activate, and then squeeze your buttocks together. Go on, squeeze those buttocks. More. Squeeze. More. Yes, lovely buttocks. And now, now you engage your abdominal muscles.
-My six pack?
-Come on, you do know how to do it, we've done this countless times.
-Have we?
-You do this, remember, by lengthening up up up through your body, stretch, stre-tch, that's it, lengthening and lifting, and then you roll your shoulder blades back and together, no, tighter, no, much tighter than that, and lift your head up. Open up your chest, open up the muscles at the top of your chest. Head up! Chin in. Mouth closed. Come on. No stooping. We don't want stooping, do we? We want the Duke of Edinburgh.

That's the sort of thing on which I now have to spend some

part of every day, fifteen minutes exercise at the very least she says, even though, as we're into telling the truth, she didn't say the words lovely buttocks. Would have been nice, though, wouldn't it?

-Good, she says.

-Really?

-Now for your balance.

-Can I sit down for a bit?

-We've only just started. Nothing is more important than your balance. Because we don't want you falling, do we? Last time you were lucky. To be honest, very lucky. You got away with it. Next time could be really nasty and we don't want that. Always make sure, so that you feel safe, make sure you are close to a chair or near a wall.

-Bit difficult if you're in an unwalled garden.

-Ready?

-Yes.

-You're not giddy?

-No.

-You're sure?

-Sure. Well, I do get a bit of a dip and a rush.

-Right. We'll keep an eye on that. Stand on one leg, can you, no, one leg, try again, don't worry about the wobble. Try again. The wobble's all part of it. Don't worry, I'll catch you. That's it, now swing your hip forwards and backwards, further back, go on, further, push yourself, don't be tentative, you have to attack everything more, you need to be less tentative as a person, Jonathan, more positive.

-No, don't tell me.

-What?

-You're going to use the word pro-active.

★

If I'm honest, I used to rather look down on physiotherapy. Come to that, and I suppose it follows, I used to rather look down on physios themselves. After all, the whole thing was to do with bodies, wasn't it, and fitness and muscles and strength and tracksuits and handstands, bodies not minds. It wasn't serious. It wasn't cerebral. I mean, you couldn't really call it a discipline, could you? Going back to my own schooldays again, for just a moment and the status that various subjects then had, Phys Ed, or PE, previously known as PT, Physical Training, or Physical Jerks, was in there with metalwork and woodwork, in there with lathes and brown overalls, with all the things that were to be later huddled together under the large umbrella of DT: Design Technology, which was one rung below Art.

I'd like to show my education and my attitude in a better, less superior light, less intellectually snobbish light, but the above is the truth, it is how things were. It is what was widely thought, if left unsaid. Anything with the word *phys* in the title was for those who didn't make the cut. Apart, of course, from Physics.

★

Imagine, if you would, that you are sitting alone in a theatre.

As the lights on the stage come up you see before you an empty space, with just a plinth in pride of place, a treatment table positioned centre stage like some kind of altar. But, as your eyes quickly adjust, you realise it is not a completely empty set: there is a long wall barre, of the sort used for exercises in ballet classes, while in the left upstage corner there is a full length moveable mirror, of the sort to be found in many a bedroom. There are also, you notice, a couple of cupboards or lockers.

And a treadmill.

The light is clean, it is functional: a hard light, an unsparing strip light which is so white it carries with it the risk of triggering a migraine. This is a physio's room. There is nothing cosy here.

There is nowhere to hide. It is stripped bare. After all, you only come to a place like this to sort out or to address or, at the very least, to ease or massage your body – to face the aches and the pains and the traumas – you come here for physiotherapy, or physio for short.

Welcome to a world of strains and breaks, knees, shoulders, hips, posture, back spasms, car accidents, whiplash, strokes, cricked necks, spinal cord injury, paralysis, all kinds of neuro rehab, neuro this neuro that, you name it, because all roads lead not to France but to Physio, to the world of Hands On.

Let me ask you, though, before we go any further, when you hear the word *physio* what do you see?

I used to see a track-suited man, or more likely two tracksuited men, it could of course these days be women but usually it's men, running from the dugout on to a football pitch to attend to a player rolling and writhing on the ground. The player looks in agony. He looks crippled. The excitable commentator hopes it's nothing too serious. Is it a hamstring or a groin, could be cramp, ankle, calf or metatarsal, is it so bad the physios will shortly be waving to the dugout and miming stretcher-bearers, while the referee (keeping one eye on his watch) is leaning over the injured man? Or, hang on, hang on a minute, is the player in his own good time slow-ly get-t-ing up and trying his foot on the turf, testing his weight on the turf before gingerly hobbling away? Is he? He is. So, was it (as many suspected) nothing much after all, nothing, just a bit of play acting, of slowing the game down, a tactic, admit it we all do it, a bit of the old nudge-nudge wink-wink, a bit of professional time-wasting?

And the physios pack up their bags and run off the pitch and the ref blows his whistle and the game restarts.

By the way, I could have done with one myself, a stretcher that is, after I recently took a header walking down the garden path. Hang on, the word *stretcher*, there's something about that word that rings a distant bell. Think. You've still got a decent memory, well, more or less. Go on, think. You can still think. It's in a novel. It's in a famous novel.

Well, Mark Twain uses *stretcher* as his word for a lie, doesn't he, in *Huckleberry Finn*, a colloquialism for those exaggerations that cross the line and stretch out into lies. It's in that wonderful opening page of Mark Twain's story. Come to think of it, *lovely buttocks* was a bit of a stretcher on my part.

No matter.

I had gone out of the kitchen door to top up the bird feeders, mainly for the tits and goldfinches, a fiddly task in which I often spill most of the niger seeds straight on to the grass, thereby providing easy pickings for the already obese pigeons. Tell you what, while we're on the topic, and very briefly, I'm fairly fed up with those waddling pigeons and their indiscriminate disease ridden droppings, leaving every foot of my garden path smeared white and grey and waiting for you to dodge it or step in it. Anyway, I was also *en route* to checking if all was ok in my writing hut, where I now more often than not find myself not writing at all, but staring straight ahead, with my head in the past, writing in my mind the books my hand will never now write, recollecting and revisiting my own spots of time, flickering in and out of focus like one of Philip Larkin's old fools.

I was wearing, as luck would have it, my big black three-quarter length winter coat, all padded, all big zips and hidden pockets, and then surprising you by even more hidden pockets, a kind of cross between a puffer and a duvet, given me last Christmas by son Ed, so that I'm fit and ready at a moment's notice for my next overland solo expedition to reach the North Pole.

It had been a cold spell in Kent and it had been unusually wet. And it was a while since I'd opened up my hut: it's one of my favourite spots in the corner of the garden, with me perched there watching the birds, feed the birds, tuppence a bag, tuppence, tuppence, tuppence a bag, Julie Andrews 1964, I was teaching in Edinburgh in 1964, or was it 1963, *I want to hold your hand* was on all day but basically I was breaking loose in jazz, as well as listening to Dinah Washington sing *September in the Rain* and *Drinking Again.*

Anyway, that's neither here nor there, the point is you can barely hear the A26 traffic from my plain hut even though the busy main road is less than fifty yards away. The hut is made of oak, and sparsely furnished, with a bookshelf and a simple table and an upright chair which faces a pencil drawing of – and words by – a melancholy Edward Thomas. (*I knew it was wrong, and that many would like it.*) And running along the top shelf there's my other Thomas, my battered Dylan Thomas paperback of *Portrait of the Artist as a Young Dog,* and my complete Chekhov (*everything I read now seems not short enough*) and there's my John Betjeman collection and Ted Hughes' letters and everything ever written by Mrs Gaskell. I've just re-read *Mary Barton,* God I do like her books. Then there's Fanny Burney, J. L. Carr, Arthur Miller, Henrik Ibsen, Paul Scott, David Lodge, George Eliot, Wendy Cope, Robert Louis Stevenson and to crown them all, Philip Larkin. (*Describing things does help to get rid of them. Hence literature.*)

From time to time I re-arrange them on the shelves in my hut, these favourite writers and their telling remarks, randomly shuffling the pack, but they're always there or thereabouts, my team, always with me, always inspiring me, and with one eye on the bird table and one eye on my hut I forgot myself – something I've been told by my physio never to do – and suddenly I was flying, and for a split second it did feel a little bit like flying, if a very short flight, no, more like a crash landing, or an aborted take-off, what the, whack, what the, thud, as if I had been picked up from behind and chucked into a concrete swimming pool head first and full length with my feet tied together.

Don't try to move.

I'd been told.

I'd been warned.

I couldn't say I hadn't been warned.

Was this to be the first fall of many?

It took me ten minutes or so to get up, or it felt like ten minutes, creaking half way up on to my left knee, trying out each limb, one by one, ankles, knees, right hip, elbows, then teeth, all there, a bit of blood on my lips, I could taste it, but the main thing was I couldn't stand up, I couldn't lift myself. I didn't have the core strength. Fuck, fuck, fuckety fuck. And it took me another ten minutes, or so it felt, my hands scuffed sore, to crawl on all fours past the flower pots and past the drain pipe and back up to the kitchen door.

Thank God for the puffer/duvet. I was lucky. Clare was right.

★

A woman walks on to our stage, carrying a cloth and a plastic bottle and, under her left arm, a big roll of paper towel. She sprays and wipes clean all the surfaces. She is doing this briskly and very thoroughly, paying particular attention first to the long wall barre and then to the plinth, wiping it top and bottom and right underneath and around the hole, around the aperture through which your nose pokes when you're lying face down on your stomach.

Finally she tears off about six feet of paper, in one long strip, shakes it out and lays it along the plinth, along the treatment table, spreading a white sheet like a table cloth, or an altar cloth, an altar pall.

Job done, she looks round to check her handiwork, looks at her watch and then calls out,

-Jonathan?

★

I have been one of Clare's clients – or, if you prefer, one of her patients – for five years now. The NHS did not offer me any physiotherapy, which I quite understand, so I had to go private and at our very first session and looking me straight in the eye she said, look, between us we can try to stop the dam breaking, we can delay things, we can settle for a pond, at least you haven't left it all too late to see me, so let's do our best, shall we, do our best to hold it all back.

I liked that. Those simple words of hers. I like simple words. I like simple sentences. And that dam image put a spring in my step, not literally of course – my springing days are long gone, as you have already seen – but I settled in straightaway for a regular session with her each fortnight. Whether I wanted to or not, I was about to learn a lot more about physio and bodies, and certainly about mine. About hands and touch. She takes my hand. Her hand is warm and strong.

Clare and I have, in a natural unforced way – me sometimes on my back, sometimes face down on the plinth, head through the hole, eyes closed, having my neck or back or shoulders or legs or ankles or whatever wonky area worked over, Clare kneeling over me – we have come to talk about many things. Life, basically. Though we are generations apart, bit by bit, over the months, over the years, by a remark here and a remark there, another tiny portion of the canvas has been coloured in. All very professionally. And then, slowly at first, even shyly, as if the topic was too private, she has started to ask me about my earlier days, things getting closer to home, and then she asked me, among other things, but quite persistently, about writing and about books, my passions.

And I, in turn, have asked her more.

She has done a lot of gutsy things in her life, Clare, taking on big physical challenges, no, not just big, taking on extreme physical challenges. It's jaw dropping stuff for a man like me. Swimming, cycling, climbing mountains, you name it.

Swimming the English channel, cycling the length of France north to south, cycling from John o' Groats to Land's End, and doing the Iron Man Triathlon. If the phrase Iron Man rings no bells with you, it is the most demanding one-day sporting event in the world, a 2.4 mile swim, followed by a 112 mile bike ride, followed by a twenty-six mile marathon, in that order and all without a break. Even typing those Iron Man figures on to the screen makes me full of wonder. Iron Woman more like. That's before her mountain climbing, for example the Munros in Scotland, for example Mont Blanc, all 15,771 feet of it. (I've climbed Pen-y-fan in the Brecon Beacons, all 2,907 feet of it.)

Oh, did I miss out Everest base camp?

As for all that, I can only imagine.

And she is, above all, totally at ease with her body, at home in her skin, as the saying goes, and on that score it still surprises me what she has done for me and my attitude to my body. And I-know-I know there is a long way to go.

–Did you get here all right? Journey ok?

–Yes, easy.

–And how's things? Generally?

–Not bad.

–But not good?

–Not too bad.

–Good. Clothes off, Jonathan, let's have a look at you.

This clothes off takes me for ever, and, every time my clumsy slow fumbling irritates the hell out of me. For a start, my unresponsive fingers. And please, if you don't mind, don't bounce straight back to me in a bright and breezy voice about how oh yes you know the feeling of being all fingers and thumbs, just don't, that's all, because there's a category difference. Do not. Laces. Laces? Ever tried tying a bow with your shoelace? Second nature, isn't it? No, it's not. It's a study in slow first gear humiliation. Buttons. Buttons? I hate them. Bloody hate them. Zips. Zips? Depends. Sometimes things go smoothly, sometimes things can get caught halfway up halfway down. Excruciating. Velcro. Velcro? *Vel* -cro! Perhaps you like hearing that shhh hushy sticky strippy rippy unpeely tearing sound, the sound of slowly undoing your shoes?

I haven't come to terms with all this, the ridiculous amount of time that every simple task takes. Not really. Not deep down. But I still don't want to admit this.

–No hurry, Clare says, without irony.

I try not to snort.

–When do I ever?

–Could you recommend a good book for me?

–Love to. Give me a second. Let me get these trousers off first.

–I'm trying to read more. And I want to support our local bookshop.

–Great. That's great, Clare.

Small pause.

–Even better, she said carefully, have you written anything yourself lately? On to anything?

–No!

Which came out more strongly than I meant.

–Nothing?

–Not a thing.

–OK. How have the exercises been going?

–A bit on and off. To be honest, not as regular as I'd like. Tell you one thing, though, Clare.

–Yes?

–I find the walking backwards exercise you suggested last time a bit tricky. Knocked a picture clean off my sitting room wall yesterday. I was backing, reversing out from the kitchen, left foot backwards first, with a bit of penguin waddle, all going nicely until my right shoulder clipped my Leonard Cohen Live in London poster.

–Bad luck.

–I must have been over-confident.

-Still, better than too timid.

-Must have been going a bit faster in reverse than I thought.

-Old but still sexy, wasn't he?

-Who?

-Leonard.

We both like Leonard Cohen. Another connection.

-Exactly, I said. He was always sexy, even as an old man. And he knew it.

-Sexy people always know they're sexy.

-You think so?

-Always.

-Perhaps I'll buy a black trilby hat like his. That might be the thing, what do you reckon? The hat might do the trick, it might, Clare, it might bring the girls running, even this late in the day.

-Concentrate more on your stretching. How's the neck?

-Better. You really helped there last time. Thanks.

-Not letting your head loll forward on your chest?

-Trying not to do that.

-But generally less stiffness? In your neck? And right shoulder?

-Definitely.

After the inventory we fell quiet for a while. Then she made another move,

-Have you thought about joining a class? We did discuss that, didn't we? A dance class. A choir. A bowls club. Whatever.

-I'm thinking about it.

-Which with you means no. You need to get out and about more. Join in more.

-The thing is, Clare, I've spent my life in classes. Once a teacher, always a teacher.

-Anyway, I still want to ask you something. I have done for a while now.

-Go on.

-You might not be keen. Especially when I've just had my head bitten off. It might seem a cheek.

-You're usually pretty persuasive.

-Well, I wondered, I was wondering, if you'd ever consider writing something again, something new. I don't know about what, you tell me. Maybe who influenced you, who caught your eye, that sort of thing.

I moved away a little, dodging eye contact, preoccupying myself with a button.

-I can't write any more. I thought I'd told you that.

-You're sure?

-I'm sure. It's flogging a dead horse, I've done my dinger.

-That's the kind of thing you always say. You never miss a chance to be bleak about yourself, do you? Why is that?

-Because it's true.

-Is it?

-Yes. I often feel ... just that.

She didn't fill the pause, until ...

-That's a pity.

-Sorry. I'd love to, but I'm finished.

-Never mind, she said. Forget it. Forget I mentioned it.

-I'd rather you told me about being a physio. That really would interest me, a bit of your professional inside track.

-I wouldn't normally, but I'll do that if you tell me about the books you like, and why you like books, and things about writers, tell me stories about writers. I'd love to know. In a way I'm playing catch-up. I've been thinking about this for a while now. Hands talk to the body and the body talks to the brain. I may have said that before, if so don't tell me. Anyway, leave the hands bit to me, let them do their talking and who knows what they might stir?

I didn't, I admit, see this one coming, I didn't expect this line of pressure.

-What sort of thing do you mean?

I'd nearly finished the undoing and the pulling off.

-Anything, she said. You come up with it.

-Anything?

-Up to you. Feel free. You're the writer.

This was annoying me.

-No. I'd rather not. Honestly.

She shrugged a little. A little unmissable shrug. And I added,

-I'll think about it.

She said nothing. And continued to say nothing.

-Look, I said I'll think about it. And I will.

She said,

-Nothing too literary, mind. Nothing too booky.

Don't be literary, darling.

Well, that was it, that was red rag to a bull. I sat up, and I was off. I could hear an old classroom voice of mine returning, I was back centre stage, overriding, assertive, my voice on the edge of command, my voice close to a rant:

-No, Clare, no, don't give me that, *nothing too booky*, that's not fair. If we get into anything new there'll be no allowances made, not on my side, none whatsoever, no allowances, no half measures, no quarter given, no dumbing down.

-OK.

She seemed to enjoy my irritation. I may have caught the hint of a private smile as I went on,

-You'll get my A game or nothing. I'm not going to muck about. You can handle it all. Easily. And anyway you've never been one to back away from a challenge yourself. How on earth did you climb Mont Blanc? How did you get to Everest base camp? How did you swim the Channel?

-I like pushing myself physically, that comes naturally to me. And, all right, I admit it, I wanted to impress.

-Anyone in particular?

-The world. Myself. A few men.

We both laughed.

-Well, I'm sure you did. You'll have done that all right.

-Right, come over to the barre.

Don't be literary, darling.

Those tantalizing words kicked in. Who wrote it, come on, come on, how did it go?

I got to my bare feet and set off.

–No. That's a bad start, Jonathan. Really bad. Head up, lift right through your body. Shoulder blades pressed together. You're tilting. That's better, don't slump. Duke of Edinburgh. Medals. Chest out.

–Bloody hell, that is bossy.

–*Pos*-ture! That's better, much better, I can hear the band. Now walk across the room again, this time with your head up, eyes up not down, keep your eyes on the middle distance. No stooping, no C position. And, berets on, now, now start swinging your arms, swing them more, up and down the room, you're leading the march past, you're leading the troops, a-bout turn, avoid the treadmill, and past the Cenotaph you go. That's it. That's smart. Look up. We're proud of you.

Don't be literary, darling.

I remember reading the poem in a magazine somewhere, it's a poem by Sasha Moorsom. It would be so cool, wouldn't it, so good for self-esteem, if I could now quote the whole poem off the cuff, that would really dazzle Clare, but as usual I can't. At best I can usually manage a few lines and then, sure enough, my confidence goes and I start the quiet slide down into muffled mumbling te-tum-te-tum-te-tumming. I've had colleagues who could quote by heart reams of Milton, Donne, Pope, Coleridge and Wordsworth. One freak, actually a very nice man, could close his eyes and recite T. S. Eliot's *The Four Quartets*, the whole damn thing. I mean, imagine that. I've never even managed to read it all the way to the end.

As for Sasha Moorsom,

Don't be literary, darling, don't be literary,
If you're James in the morning you're Hemingway in bed,

Don't talk of yourself in the style of your own obituary –
For who cares what they say of you after you're dead.

Don't be always a thought ahead and a move behind
Like a general reconnoitring dangerous ground,
This is a game it's much better to enter blind
And the one who wins is the one who is caught and bound.

If you can't be straight then just say nothing instead.
I'll know what you mean much better than if it was said.

Sasha Moorsom (1931–1993)

Anyway that is how, most unexpectedly, although it took me
an unsettled week of bad nights and false starts, that is how the
concept of the lost chapters started to grow: I was back in the
classroom, back in my classroom, saying whatever I wanted to
say, enjoying the self-indulgent teacher's monologue, and starting
my lessons wherever I wanted to start. In one sense, although
it was initially against my wishes, I knew I had already begun
revisiting my own *spots of time*, those renovating moments of
one's life, those small memorable moments which can sometimes
lift us up when we are fallen, even repair us, an idea nicked, of
course, as you will probably know, from Wordsworth's *Prelude*.

But I did not tell Clare that I was launched. I did not say what
I was up to, let alone say that all the pieces were being written
for her. The cat stayed for a while in the bag. Instead of coming
clean I went under the radar, crawling under the wire. I kept my
head down, writing a few pages here and a few paragraphs there,
in secret, like a spy, like a guilty Albert Speer scribbling away in
his Spandau prison cell, *Herr* Speer, telling no one of his interior
journey, of his world walk. Sometimes I do that. It excites me.

So, spots of time.

I was going to start with something on Dylan Thomas and

Kingsley Amis. I was going to start with something teenage, a teenage memory, something set on that summer's day in Swansea in 1958, but then I thought no, first up it's got to be on books, on books in general, on books full stop. I had to go straight in at the deep end.

Typing with one finger on my good hand, and with a pulse of energy, I was off.

★

King Lear

I've never liked rows and I do my best to avoid them, believing that far from clearing the air they usually make things worse, but some rows are unavoidable, and when I was twenyt-three I had an upsetting one, one I have never forgotten.

It was with a university friend who asked me what on earth gave me the idea that I knew enough to edit Shakespeare's *King Lear*, or, let alone that, *Othello*. That morning I had been offered the chance by a publisher to edit one Shakespeare tragedy or the other, it was my choice, and what a choice, so I hurried round to tell my friend the good news. He would be pleased for me.

Over a cup of tea I said that it was nice to think that my name was going to be in print for the first time on a book cover and, what's more, right next to Shakespeare's. OK, they're only paying a pittance, I said, barely enough to keep me in beer and fags, but it's not a bad start. I was being facetious, as we often were with each other, and that may have been what did it, but it's more likely something else was the cause, something that had long been brewing. I don't know.

Anyway, he threw his cup and his saucer at me and he roared, *What do you know about suffering? What the hell do you know about sexual jealousy?* Then he stood up and grabbed my cup and saucer. For a second or two I thought he was going to attack me, but he was now throwing them full pelt straight at the wall, first the cup, then the saucer. Then the half full bottle of milk shattered. The last thing I heard him screaming as I ran from his room was ...

All you ever do is read books! Come back here! What do you know about life!

★

In 1975, I saw Simon Gray's comedy *Otherwise Engaged* on the stage in London. It was directed by Harold Pinter, and starred Alan Bates, Nigel Hawthorne and (in later years to become a friend of mine) Benjamin Whitrow. The central character of the play is a wittily defensive and coldly selfish publisher, Simon Hench, who is planning to spend a comfortable four hours listening to a new recording of Wagner's *Parsifal,* only to find he is constantly interrupted by a string of people with demands or claims on his time. One by one they disturb him. One by one he shows them to the door: his school teacher brother, his lodger, a journalist, an old school friend, and finally his wife. She arrives to tell him that she is leaving him, that she is pregnant, that she has a lover and it may be her lover's child.

Hench can't wait to get back to Wagner and *Parsifal.*

★

books (i)

Most of my life has been spent with books and with people who read – with reading people – with people for whom reading is either important or almost everything: with those who love, if not live for, literature, those who take their daily pleasure in books and who feel bereft without them. Though it is often taken as a disparaging phrase, Clare, in some ways you could say

I have led a bookish life.

Not that it feels like that.

It feels much more like falling in love over and over again. One day, without consciously looking for her, you come across a writer new to you, or someone points her out – it could be a man, it could be a woman, but a muse is female and I'm a man so I'm calling her a woman – and suddenly everything is different. You catch her eye. You start to circle the table on which she lies, even the shelf on which she sits. You find your moment and you reach out. Yes, you like her.

Have another look. Don't rush.

Yes, she's got it. In no time at all, back you go again. You want to find out more about her. Then, it happens so quickly, you can't get enough of her. You can't wait to see her again, the way the sun lights up the sky. And you can't keep your hands off. You need more of the same, or more of something different as long as it is more of her. She speaks to me like no one else. You hardly sleep. Why would I sleep in her company? You want her with you all the time, on the train, on the bus, on holiday, in bed. I see everything in a different way, you say to yourself. She's bright, she's deep. This is different. She stirs you. You laugh and cry together. How did you ever live without this experience?

Or …

Or, one day the thought steals up on you that something isn't quite right, it isn't working. Have you been taken in? Did you misread her? No, you don't want to face it. You check back. Now you're worried. You suspect that she knows how to capture you, how to hook you, how to make the first few chapters go, but not how to hold you as you go on together. Was it just her sexy style you fell for, the clever look, the fetching literary dress, her manner, the latest tone, the latest wave, and you gradually realise, and you don't you really don't want to admit this to yourself let alone to your friends, because you've banged on about her for so long, you don't want to admit that you now realise that there wasn't much *there*, not much substance, not much heart.

And so you go on … through all the stages of partnership and commitment, devotion, settling in for the long haul, a lifelong friendship, occasional disillusionment, it's now a bit samey, a break-up, a getting together again, is it a final parting of the ways or a rapprochement, who knows how it will end, time will tell, no, as Auden says, time will say nothing but I told you so.

No, *a bookish life* does sound a bit dull, doesn't it, if not as off-putting as *being a bookworm*. The phrase 'a bookish life' carries a clearly pejorative edge, smacking of a studiously retiring addiction, if not of life-evasion or life-avoidance, which at the very least is likely to lead to pedantry or taciturnity. Halfway up a book ladder, with your knees resting on a rung and your head stuck in a dusty tome, how can you ever build up much knowledge of 'the wonderful wide world waiting for you out there', not to mention mountains to climb? You're in danger of becoming a Dr Casaubon: Dr Edward Casaubon, the dry-as-a-stick middle-aged clergyman in *Middlemarch*, who fruitlessly pursues a scholarly (no, a boring) topic, while neglecting Dorothea, his vibrant, idealistic and intelligent young wife.

A book cannot, and should not – as Kafka says – take the place of the world. How can you be in a library all day, wedged in a carrel desk, wasting your time to no purpose when all this while you are living – or should be really living – with a woman like Dorothea? The end result, as Dr Leavis put it, is that for both of them marriage is a form of solitary confinement.

I would, however – despite the futility of Dr Casaubon, despite his cautionary example – argue that reading has carried me away to new places and down open roads and into the byways; that it has given me insights and 'experiences' which I have taken with me into my wider life, insights and experiences that have helped me to read it.

There is, it seems to me, no conflict of interest between life and books. Flaubert said in 1857 we 'read in order to live.'

And you take that understanding with you into your everyday experience, an understanding which may well change with each re-reading because with words, as we know, there is no such thing as 'the last word'.

★

one toe at a time

-Can you loosen up my feet, d'you think?

-Your feet?

-Wake them up a bit, would you? They don't want to move.

-Let's have a look.

-They're lazy, leaden, uncooperative sods with a mind of their own.

-Well, you've made that clear enough.

-No, that's not it, it's worse, they have no mind. They're dead. Stiffs.

-Are you finding it more difficult putting your shoes on?

-Yes. And my underpants. I get into a comic tangle, hanging on to the heated towel rail, with both legs in one opening, if that's vivid enough for you.

-Right.

-Some days they're worse than others, the feet. The right one's worst. And, as you know, I like to give you new challenges.

She bent down close to my feet as I sat on the narrow plinth, my legs dangling over the side.

-How does that feel, Jonathan?

-What?

-What I just did.

-I didn't feel you do anything.

-OK. Let's see what we can do. Lie back. Careful. Giddy?

-No.

-Let's take it one toe at a time, shall we?

I slowly settled down on my back, lowering my head on to a small pillow, one of those hard small ones favoured by dentists, and she started to massage and work my toes, toe by toe, working away, bringing them back to a bit of life. My blood seemed about to flow, or at least to set off on its rather reluctant roundabout journey, round the extremities, or as Churchill put it, round the back streets. I closed my eyes and gave in to it. Yes. There was something, definitely, a sensation of sorts in my big toes. There was life in me yet.

–Don't get too comfy, will you, because after this we'll be doing some lunges and ta-dahs. And the skate board.

–Oh, good, my forte.

–We need to get you going.

–Don't you worry, I'm ready to explode.

She began to press harder, and forcefully flex my feet up and down and sideways, left, right, up, down, round and round, pressing more strongly.

–Tell me, I've forgotten, how many years did you teach?

–Forty. A lifetime in the classroom.

–Did you move around the country? From school to school?

–No, not much, a bit, I was thirty-five years in the same place.

–Wow, you must have liked it, the school you taught at.

–I did. Yes, I did.

–You were happy?

–I was, mostly. But not too doggone happy. I'm a bit wary of all that 'I'm so happy' stuff. How does it go? Be happy, kid, but not too happy, not happy happy, be happy, but not too doggone happy, kid, because the happy happy do bust hard when they bust.

–Who's that?

–An American. Carl Sandburg, it's a poem by him, or getting close to it.

–And your own schooldays? Were you unhappy?

–Me? Not sure. More interestingly, was E.M. Forster?

–Jonathan?

A new tone. A silent perusal.

–Mmnnhh?

–Just wanted to ask. Again.

–Ask away.

–Whether you've –

–What?

I opened one eye, half lifting my head.

–Been up to anything interesting?

–Not really. Bit of this and that. Mostly pottering around in the garden, to be honest.

–Is that your version of being honest?

–Yes.

–I've never seen you as the pottering around the garden type.

–And I'm into the latest Sebastian Barry novel. He's got it, he really has, it's his voice, his take. Another Irish genius. They're absolutely everywhere, you know, these brilliant Irish writers, it's a scandal, an epidemic.

–Sebastian who? Never heard of him. Is that terrible?

–Afraid so.

I closed my eyes again, bringing this thread to an end. There was, though, something different about her. Not her voice exactly. What was it, was it a new haircut? Could be. She was the last person to draw attention to herself. Anyway, I didn't want to say anything in case I got it wrong, or struck too personal a note, or in case it was quite simply another of my misreadings. Don't be personal, dear, my mother used to say, never make personal remarks.

After a few more minutes she asked,

–How are the ankles? And the feet?

–Like new.

What the hell, go for it.

–Great haircut, Clare.

–Thanks. Time for a change, I thought. So, now something

new for you, time for some lunges. You'll love practising these. Stand firmly on one foot and lunge forward with the other foot. But come up slowly, sit up, take all the time you need. Don't worry, trust me, I'm here if you wobble. You might be a bit swimmy, a bit whooshy. Let's see. No, you're fine. Tough guy.

★

Read anything good lately?

What a great start to a conversation that is, Clare, what a chat-up line, and such a simple move towards the intimacy which two imaginations and a shared hinterland can bring. To a reader, the world and the book are indivisible, so much so that when we experience something for the first time in life we often feel we have experienced it before, 'been there before, seen it, done it'. *You ghost into a book in silent perusal* (these phrases again, I have read these phrases before, some years ago now, but I cannot recall where. Is it Italo Calvino, yes, they're borrowings, yes, it's him, it's in his *Why read the classics*? I'll track them all down later) and you save and store the voices and faces of the past. Even if not fully understood at the time, the voices and the faces enter the life of our minds. And in that sense we *have* 'been there, we have seen it, we have done it,' because we have encountered and lived inside a similar scene in a book. And the book felt real.

Books can, then, get you there first. Even a chance meeting in life can feel like a chance meeting with a new writer, a writer new to you, that is.

Tell you what, changing tack a bit, and I've never said this before –

In the years since I left the full-time classroom behind, I have come to admit to myself how much more of my career I spent thinking in a very specific manner about each of my pupils, trying to *read them* rather than setting prep/homework or marking their essays. *Thinking about them* or *reading them* rang truer and more important to me than conventionally charting or assessing their progress, because their eyes were everything.

Look into their eyes, I told myself. Look into the eyes of your pupils. As I know you do with your physio patients, look into the eyes of a book. Read there: read a face for signs as one reads the sky for a coming storm or learns to see patterns in ceaseless Cornish waves. For example, the bully's eyes were everything. As were the eyes of the vulnerable. Not to mention the look in the eye of the pupil who is turning a corner or intellectually taking off.

Oh, and walking. Read their walking. Or, at a push, in your case, read their mountain climbing.

Even the way my pupils walked away from me or walked past me often said more to me about how they were getting on than their written work.

Quite often, particularly if things were not going well, particularly if I was feeling a lack of rapport with my classes, I would spend half an hour or so alone in my room, not scribbling in red ink on their essays or even planning my lessons (don't be silly), but looking at their names in an alphabetical list in my mark book (which was, in truth, pretty thin on what you might call the old actual mark front) because running my eye down the names interested me much more and subconsciously shaped how I taught. I think I was trying to read between their lines, to pick up their body language, trying to see deeper into them, trying to hear what was being unsaid and trying to decipher the unwritten:

> *Your face, my Thane, is as a book*
> *Where men may read strange matters.*
> We often say of people,
> *He's an open book.*
> or
> *She's a closed book.*

Presumptuous? Perhaps. Amateur psychology? Perhaps. And of course, in many instances with my pupils, I didn't have a mortal clue what was going on in their minds and in their hearts and I could well have been miles off track. I have misread many books. I have misread many people. I have got so much wrong.

But reading them is what I did, or at least is what I tried to do. That was my approach: the book, the teacher, the pupil, the reader, the writer were all one, and books were the meeting point where we enjoyed (often without admitting it) the secluded parts of ourselves. That is why I always felt reading lessons were important in a school week, those lessons in which all the pupils in the class silently read whatever book they choose. Something important, I often sensed, can happen in those silent sessions, something mute, something un-taught but caught, something that matters more than everyone talking for the sake of talking. In some ways an authoritative statement is being made about what endures: something collective is, I sense, being felt between readers individually 'lost' yet held together in another world, warmly, in a kind of unspoken alliance.

And my reading, my knowledge gained from books, fed into everything, an extension of my sympathy. From an early age I got 'lost' in books myself, as readers do, books that at the time may well have been too deep for me, and escaped, armed with them, into life.

What happens to us after those readings in which we lose ourselves? How do we read our own lives, and the lives of the people we know, the people who don't know what we have just read, or understood?

Reading takes you out of yourself and into new versions of your self, because reading makes you question the very notion of a single self. Reading makes it more difficult for you to stay content to be one person, as you find you are provoked or converted or altered or unbalanced or divided or dislocated by the unexpected. In my favourite jazz phrase, while reading books *you break loose.*

And, last point, to help me in my reading of life and literature I have always loved watching the faces of actors on the stage or on the screen or in a radio studio, seeing what their eyes say, hearing what their bodies whisper, watching their eyes, *watch their eyes*, half-catching this brief snatch of half-heard dialogue, that unfinished sentence. In particular I have always watched how actors deliver the unspoken soliloquy, all those giveaway bits of life and art, the invisible ink that doesn't get into the written screenplay.

★

suddenly standing up

One night I woke up, pitch black outside, and I was soon at my desk, writing out a list. The missing chapters. I did not plan or impose any order on the names. They took up their place in the line like soldiers falling in on a parade ground.

Sasha Moorsom
Kingsley Amis and Dylan Thomas
Arthur Miller
Wordsworth and George Eliot
J.L.Carr
Brian Moore
Robert Louis Stevenson and W.E.Henley
Lord Moran
Albert Speer
Wendy Cope
Elizabeth Jennings
Charlotte Mew
E.M.Forster
Charlotte Charke

Anthony Powell
Christina Rossetti
Owen Sheers

After I'd finished writing those names, typing them with one finger, I sat for a while then stood up, lost in my thoughts, and I stood up too quickly. I should, as I've been told countless times, stand up carefully and stretch and walk about a bit every half hour or so. When I remember to do so I put the kitchen timer on to buzz me, but if I forget myself, if I'm engrossed, and feeling private and secret inside my head, as I was on books, as I was while writing this, it's then that I do stupid things. And it's then I lose my control and balance and risk injury.

I stood there swaying and clawing the air and reaching out for the mantelpiece, for support, but it soon started to clear, and I found myself shaking less if I thought of that Wendy Cope cricket and King Lear poem. She always cheers me up.

The Cricketing Versions

(for Simon Rae)

There isn't much cricket in the Cromwell play
(overheard at a dinner party)

There isn't much cricket in *Hamlet* either,
There isn't much cricket in *Lear*,
I don't think there's any in Paradise Lost –
I haven't a copy right here.

But I like to imagine the cricketing versions –
Laertes goes out to bat
And instead of claiming a palpable hit,
The prince gives a cry of 'Howzat!'

While elsewhere the nastier daughters of Lear
(Both women cricketers) scheme
To keep their talented younger sister
Out of the England team,

And up in the happy realms of light
When Satan is out (great catch)
His team and the winners sit down together
For sandwiches after the match,

Although there are some English writers,
Who feature the red leather ball,
You could make a long list of the plays and the books
In which there's no cricket at all.

To be perfectly honest, I like them that way –
The absence of cricket is fine.
But if you prefer work that includes it, please note
That now there's some cricket in mine.

Wendy Cope (1945 -)

★

Clare does not muck about. Within minutes of me arriving
at her clinic she is working on my body. She has all the gifts,
and she works hard and I'm sure much of it comes naturally,
but I can also see she is assessing me, am I better or worse today,
am I any different, have I been lazy, changing tack as she goes,
reading my facetious evasions, checking that I have put into
practice what we agreed last time, and never ever allowing me
off the hook.

Let me try to capture her. Her voice.

Feet feet feet feet feet feet FEET

Practise stomping and marching. Make your feet more aware, feel your toes in your shoes, because you need them for your balance. Tell your brain to use your feet, to feel them. Really feel them. You're quite well educated. Use your brain.

Talk to your feet, Jonathan.

Don't be too reliant on your arms.

Your body is stooping more because it feels safer to you that way, because you're closer to the ground, with not so far to fall, safer in a more flexed position. Am I right? Well, don't do it. Go the other way. Risk a wobble. Stand tall.

Tall tall tall tall tall TALL

Walk Tall, look the world right in the eye.

Use that balance pad you've got. Step on it and off it in your bare feet.

Do it now.

On and off it, on it and off it. Pick your feet up. Don't scuff the pad. Don't clip the ground. Step forwards and backwards and sideways, forwards and backwards and sideways. Try the penguin waddle. Better still, dance it. You'll feel wobbly. Put ABBA on. Dancing Queen. That's good, that means you're stimulating your balance reactions. Have some support nearby.

Moving on …

Do some purposeful walking and striding out. Head up. This will help you regain your confidence. Use the full length mirror in your bedroom. Check you are upright, or as upright as you can be. Imagine you are talking to an audience. You've done that a lot, haven't you? Thousands of times. I've asked around. I've checked up on you. Look outwards not downwards. Be confident in your own body. Head up.

–Clare?

–What?

–Tell me about your school days.

–I knew you weren't listening. You switch off and hide behind politeness. You get that middle distance look.

-I can't help my face. Frozen features. It's one of the symptoms.

I was in my shorts. She was kneeling at the far end of the plinth, with her arms round a large red bouncy balloon, a balloon made of thick-skinned rubber and about the size of an old fashioned medicine ball, but of course much lighter. I was now switched on, pressing as hard as I could with both my feet into the centre of the balloon, feeling the strain in my knees, pushing really hard, push push push as hard as I could, which force she was resisting. She was strong.

-Lovely legs, she said.

-Thanks, I said. You were going to tell me something.

-About how I got into all this, yes. But, no, I want to know about *your* school days. In Wales, wasn't it? Swansea?

-Another time for that. You must have been sporty at school?

-Yes, good at netball, and tennis, I was in all the teams. But I got poor marks in written tests.

-Badly taught?

-Not particularly.

-But not caught?

-More that I wasn't ready.

-Did that upset you? The exams, the poor marks?

-What do you imagine? I wasn't a thicko, I got things quickly.

-Very, I bet.

-I was physical, an active girl in the gym.

-Dancing? Ballet?

-Not specially. I liked running and climbing. And when I left school all I wanted was to be involved in games, any games. Sports physiotherapy offered me that world, at King's in London, but I soon realised that meant I was always going to be on the touchline, watching not playing, not much more really than a spectator.

-So you switched to neuro?

-I did.

-And?

-Everything was different, and my life was a thousand times more interesting.

-Great.

-I was dealing with extremes.

(You guessed. Of course you did. She didn't say it. *Lovely legs* was a stretcher.)

★

books (iii)

The physical book itself has an important life of its own, too, because readers come to love not just the words on the page but the actual physical thing itself. A book is, or should be, a beautiful thing. While you should not 'judge a book by its cover', I do judge a book by more than the sum total of its words. It is not just the words on the page.

Beauty is important: the format, the particular edition, the size of the print, the font, the breadth of the margin, the feel and thickness of the paper, the spine, even the smell of the book – no, not *even* the smell, especially the smell. In *Summoned by Bells* John Betjeman says the same. That's why, whatever the convenience of ebooks, I prefer to stay with companionable paper and firm spines, something I can touch and run my hands over and be comfortable with, something to nestle up to and to settle down with.

So I can't read (i.e. I won't read because I wouldn't enjoy) books with print too small, with margins too narrow and with far too many words crammed on each and every page. Over-crowding a page in an off-putting way strikes me as much a matter of bad manners as of style and aesthetics.

Of course a book doesn't have to be beautiful in a pristine way. It may have grown old and lost its looks. It may be battered but, like Betjeman's teddy bear Archibald Ormsby Gore, still mean a lot to us simply because it is ours, albeit dog-eared, falling apart and coffee-stained. It means a lot to us because we can remember where we bought it, where we first read it, or who gave it us, or who we were in love with at the time. It has always been on our shelves, this battered old friend, it has been with us loyally for many years and always will be. We like to know it is there. It never gets taken to Oxfam or to the doctors' waiting room or to the pub shelf and somehow it always escapes impulsive trips to the tip. People who aren't bookish just don't get this. One very clever colleague I taught with – on hearing me complain over lunch that my home was almost sagging under the weight of my hardback books – suggested I just keep the dust jackets. She wasn't joking. There are some very thick clever people.

While we reading people may be surrounded, if not submerged, by inanimate yet breathing books, we are also alive inside them and carry them around inside us. As a teacher and a writer, I admit that I have also spent much of my time trying to read people, a parallel activity on a parallel track, though (when I put it like that) it may come across as a presumptuous and impertinent claim. It may sound absurd even to make the point in the first place, to segue from books to people, let alone to try to make something of it.

After all, don't we all try to do that? That surely is a crucial aim of common humanity, to develop our sensitivity to others' feelings, to try to step into another person's shoes, to get on to their wavelength. Nevertheless, for me the two have been urgently and intimately linked. Reading books/reading people has been at the core of everything that matters to me, Clare, and reading great books helps us, I believe, to read life in a sharper and yet more generous way.

And if that could happen to me, it would follow, or it might follow, that I would become a better teacher and a better father, because there are few better ways of communicating with children, with the young, than through books. It is shared and it can work on so many levels and it can be a revelation. Once children are serious readers, their hair is endlessly ruffled by a new breeze. It's a way of 'saying' difficult and interesting things without saying them, of learning without obviously being taught, of opening the world up, of giving them a password and a passport, of allowing things to be found, of their 'coming across' life in the imagination, and all this comes about through the medium of a book.

I used to place all kinds of books on my daughter's bed, and later on my son's bed, from Edward Lear's *The Quangle Wangle's Hat* to Thackeray's *Vanity Fair*, from *Treasure Island* to *Jane Eyre*. Instead of lecturing the young or moralising too much, I was hoping it would prove better if they were 'allowed' to find themselves in a poem or story, to see other paths ahead, to work things out for themselves and possibly to think things through – all through a book.

Then leave them alone.

It may be we put a 'classic' novel – a demanding novel – in their way, a Brontë, a Thackeray, a Dickens, a James, a Woolf, a Lawrence, one that doesn't come too easily. Mind you, even compulsory reading in school can have life-changing rewards. 'For it is the destiny of those grave, restrained and classic writers,' Robert Louis Stevenson said, 'with whom we make enforced and often painful acquaintanceship at school, to pass into the blood and become native in the memory, so that a phrase of Virgil speaks not so much of Mantua or Augustus, but of English places and the student's own irrevocable youth.'

★

The door frames are, I find, narrower these days.

★

Kingsley Amis and Dylan Thomas

A few weeks back, you asked about me being young, and I didn't want to answer. I wasn't sure I could do it. Well … in we go.

Swansea, with its 'long and splendid-curving shore', has always been important to me. It was, partly, where I 'grew up', or felt that I did. Not that I ever lived there, and I probably didn't even stay there more than a dozen times, all in my mid to late teens, but those visits felt important then and they feel important now. It is not the amount of time you spend in the place that matters, it's the intensity of the experience. On some days you grow up more than you do in a decade.

It was the school summer holidays. This was 1958, I think. Arriving at Swansea High Street railway station, as it then was, you knew it was the end of the line. And it felt happily like the end of the line. It felt like Penzance does in West Cornwall, or like Padstow did in North Cornwall, like the last track on the Traveling Wilburys album does, it feels right when you're on the freight train and George Harrison is leading the singing, and there's Jeff Lynne, and Tom Petty is doing the choruses and Roy Orbison is memorably in the mix but it's all right, well it's all right, it's the end of the line, it's all right, it's the end of the line, we're coming to the end of the line, and you reach up and you get your suitcase down from the luggage rack and you drink in the sea air …

I'm here … and, as I walk out of Swansea station, I'm grown up. I'm your man.

I'm back, and I'm staying in West Cross, or maybe Pennard, clambering over the slippery rocks with my school friends Michael and Blondie, both Swansea boys, and I'm jumping on the Mumbles railway (to be honest, more of a tramway), wandering around Oystermouth Castle, talking to girls at the bus stop, there's brave, looking down from the dunes on to

Oxwich Bay or heading on further out for Rhossili, the rhythm of our walking in tune with the rhythm of our words and the bushes are brimming with blackbirds.

Michael was playing imaginary golf shots and Blondie was taking on the Australian fast bowlers, smiting them to all parts for fours, then there's me sitting on a sharp rock smoking and secretly longing to be snapped in profile, who's got a camera then, with a cigarette in my fingers, exhaling, soulful and sad, and Ireland's just across there, boys. Ireland, where my dad was striding out with his walking stick and his Edward Thomas haversack, he went with his friend in the 1920s, walking all across Ireland, all on foot, Cork, Kerry, right on round to Connemara, right, it's getting chilly, boys, and my bum's hurting, better get back to town because later I would be kissing a girl non-stop for two hours in the Tivoli cinema, occasionally catching sight of a scene from *A Summer Place* (shocking events at a summer resort) or were we seeing a re-run of *From Here to Eternity* (1953) with me and Burt Lancaster (me mostly) kissing Deborah Kerr on the beach, that was hot, but it didn't matter if I missed bits of the film because we could stay in our double seats at the back and watch it go round and round again. If you wanted you could spend all day in the cinema. They let you. Nobody seemed to mind.

> Jenny kiss'd me when we met,
>   Jumping from the chair she sat in;
> Time, you thief, who love to get
>   Sweets into your list, put that in!
> Say I'm weary, say I'm sad,
>   Say that health and wealth have missed me,
> Say I'm growing old, but add
>   Jenny kiss'd me.

Leigh Hunt (1784-1859)

Anyway the thing is, in 1958, one rainy August lunchtime, I saw the poet and novelist Kingsley Amis standing at the bar of the Newton Inn, Mumbles. He was making a group of men laugh, which was one of his gifts. He was a brilliant mimic. I whispered to my friend Blondie,

-That's Kingsley Amis.

-Who's he?

-The *Lucky Jim* bloke.

-Never heard of him.

-That's all right, you're ignorant.

-So, what does he do for a living?

-He's a writer, for God's sake.

-That all?

Kingsley Amis was a lecturer in English at Swansea University, with a reputation for *Lucky Jim* (1954), for heavy drinking and for going way beyond kissing girls. In the Newton Inn, Mumbles, in his late thirties, Amis was handsome and assured in a dangerous way. Three years later he was a don at Peterhouse, Cambridge, when I was reading English at St John's, but I never saw him around the place, though he had a reputation for *Lucky Jim*, for heavy drinking at High Table and for going way beyond kissing girls. When he fell asleep, shagged out on a Swansea beach (I read about this later) his first wife, Hilly, took her lipstick out of her handbag and wrote on his back, in big capitals (which I'll spare you, the bold capitals that is) I Fuck Anything. There's a photo to prove it.

Not that I was looking for Kingsley Amis in Swansea; I just came across him. I was looking for Dylan Thomas, as you could probably tell from my style in that long paragraph which started two pages back and which you feared would never end: Dylan Thomas, the Rimbaud of Cwmdonkin Drive, who died of drink a few years earlier, in 1953, in New York.

Swansea was Dylan.

Dylan was Swansea.

Still is, really.

I stood outside 5 Cwmdonkin Drive, a red brick semi in the

Uplands where he lived, but standing in the road there I felt very little emotion of any kind. I then stood outside Swansea Grammar School on Mount Pleasant, where Dylan Marlais Thomas was an unsuccessful pupil and where his father D.J. Thomas was, like me, an English teacher (only he got a first), but again I didn't feel much. It was what Dylan was 'up to' I was after, not looking at the house he lived in or the Grammar school to which he went.

What Dylan got up to, I now see, is best found in the ten short stories which make up his *Portrait of the Artist as a Young Dog*. I think you'd like them, Clare. Published in 1940, all the stories are set in Swansea, but I had not read much, if any, of Thomas's prose when I was a teenager. His poetry, not his prose, was the thing. That was where his glamour lay, that's where the romance was, and when I won a prize at school I selected *The Collected Poems of Dylan Thomas, 1934-1952*, to the disappointment, if not the disapproval, of my English teacher, who was an Auden man. Dylan Thomas was show biz, big show biz in the '50s, and some were suspicious of all that. Was he high-blown bullshit? But the very titles of his poems, or the first lines if there weren't any titles, arrested me. Here is a sample:

The force that through the green fuse drives the flower

Light breaks where no sun shines

And death shall have no dominion

The hunchback in the park

In my craft or sullen art

The hand that signed the paper

A Refusal to Mourn the Death, by Fire, of a Child in London

I did not read his stories, his prose, with any attention (if at all) until I became a schoolteacher in the early 1960s, and having done so I immediately ordered a set of them, deciding on the spot that I was going to teach the stories to my class the next week. That was in the days, of course, the 1960s, when you could still teach whatever books you liked, in the days before the skies darkened and the helicopters came chopping over, flying in formation, before the parachutists landed with their assessment forms and guns and pamphlets telling you what to do, listing all the bullet points that had to be made in an essay if you wanted high marks, if you wanted an A, that is, or an A★, nothing less would do, and instructing the teachers in what to look for and how to mark it. The Teacher As Story Teller was replaced by Teacher All Bases Covered.

In the Spring Term in 1969, some years before the invasion, I taught James Joyce's *Dubliners* and Dylan Thomas's *Portrait of the Artist as a Young Dog* and Siegfried Sassoon's trilogy *The Complete Memoirs of George Sherston*, and as far as I can remember nobody ever asked me what any of it was 'for'.

The Dylan Thomas *Portrait* collection explores – in a wistful, forgiving, affectionate, strong, generous but unblinking spirit – the world of growing up, particularly the messy male teenage years. Or Dylan Thomas's teenage years. And, more immediately to the point, mine.

Dylan Thomas caught youth. He had a nose for it. He caught it all: the attitudinising, the mischievous strutting, youthfulness coursing with blood, youth arrogantly alive, the self-dramatising isolation, hugging loneliness, the self-pitying sitting in the shadows of your failure, the sexual fantasies and the phoney conquests and the melodramatic late night philosophising under dark railway arches, your body an adventure, and the bragging and the embroidered anecdotes and the mythologizing and the crucial angle of the fag in your mouth, yet there was always a detached bit, a bit watching, the artist, and you were a sharp enough observer to spot the dart holes in the nose of the bitter drinker.

Being sharp matters in Wales.

Being quick.

It's the same obsession we have in rugby with outside halves, with the players in the Number 10 shirt.

Are they *quick*? Are they sharp? Have they 'got it'?

We don't want cart horses, do we? We don't want plodders.

As I read those stories, and I re-read them in my garden hut last week, re-read them for you, I was up to no good boyo again with Dylan:

> I felt all my young body like an excited animal surrounding me, the torn knees bent, the bumping heart, the long heat and depth between the legs, the sweat prickling in the hands, the tunnels down to the eardrums, the tucked-up voice, the blood racing, the memory around and within flying, jumping, swimming and waiting to pounce ... I was aware of me myself in the exact middle of the living story, and my body was my adventure and my name.

The collection of stories, conceived over a pint, begins and ends in drink. We start our journey with a curly haired little boy left sitting alone on a horse and cart outside the pub with his uncle up to no good inside, changing soon into the cheeky boy, to the five foot eight stone youth, changing to the turbulent young man reaching for the bottle – *Old Garbo* begins with him meeting an older reporter in a lavatory – to the self-destructive pub-crawling man, awash with drink, the brilliantly blotto boyo now in ruins, swaying in and out of all the dives all over Swansea.

> I liked the taste of beer, its live, white lather, its brass-bright depths, the sudden world through the wet brown walls of the glass, the tilted rush to the

lips and the slow swallowing down to the lapping belly.

In his crisp *Memoirs* (1991) Kingsley Amis gives an account of his only meeting with Dylan Thomas. It was a spring evening in 1951. Dylan Thomas had been invited to give a talk to the English Society in the Students' Union at Swansea University. In the pub beforehand, when Dylan was apathetic, Amis noticed the guest speaker slipping a couple of bottles of beer in his pockets and more than once checking that they were still there. (It takes an alcoholic to spot one.) Later, a baleful presence facing his audience, with his voice magnificent but disconcerting, Dylan ends by reading in a tremulous whisper a poem of WB Yeats: a performance, Amis said, which was 'bloody awful, a piece of naked showing-off and an insult to poetry.'

It is clear that Kingsley Amis thought Dylan Thomas a poety-poet with the gift of the gab, albeit a grandiloquent gab. Amis thought Dylan Thomas was all compound adjectives and impressionistic maundering and over-indulged puns. He thought him one of those professional Welshmen with biblical cadences and sonorous phrases, with a taste for the naughty, with a slap of the sea here and a tickle of the sand there.

And there is some force in these accusations.

In his *Memoirs,* however, Kingsley Amis goes further, much further, indulging that nasty tone which poisoned his later fiction and soured his life, describing Dylan Thomas as 'an outstandingly unpleasant man, one who cheated and stole from his friends and peed on their carpets.' That may be the case, I don't know where he peed, but peeing or not peeing, Thomas was a greater talent than his disparaging detractor, and it takes a particularly unpleasant man to write those words, especially one who himself knew only too well the tilted rush and the slow swallowing.

By the way, while on this topic and this poet, Philip Larkin, a close friend of Amis, made a more telling and perceptive remark: 'In fact, and I know it's absurd to say so, but I should say I had more in common with Dylan Thomas than any other "famous writer".'

★

–You're suggesting I stand on that?

I was looking at a thin piece of wood with four wheels under it.

–My skateboard? I am.

–Blimey.

–I want to try something with you.

–Really?

–Put your right foot on it. Step on the skateboard. Go on.

–All right.

–And keep your left foot on the ground. Firmly.

–Like that?

–Exactly. Now roll the board backwards and forwards but with your left foot planted. Don't move that foot. No, you moved it. That's it. Don't say you can't. Go on. Great. See, you can do it. You can do a lot more than you think. Hold your shape. Hang on, give me a second, let's take a photo of you. Yes, look, here you are. That's nice. Good posture, yes?

And she held out her mobile for me to see myself.

Oh, God.

In an almost instantaneous connection, in my mind's eye I was roller-skating. I was on the uneven pavements on the outskirts of bomb-damaged Bristol, not far from the city centre – this would be 1951 – but a little scared to have strayed so far from home, and all this without telling my mother where I had gone. I had gone past the roundabout, my normal boundary limit, past the airfield, past the laundry, the bank, the dentist, the cinema, self-conscious on my clumsily stiff skates, and occasionally laughed at (hey, son, call that skating?) as I turned round and laboured back up Gloucester Road past the swimming pool, or did we call it the public swimming bath, crossing the road to give the pool or bath a very wide berth because of the polio scare around swimming baths and the looming threat of an iron lung. Someone on Hempton Lane, across the road from us, had polio. That's what they said. As for an iron lung, the prospect terrified me, the thought of being encased for ever and a day in a huge metal box.

Push on, push on, put the swimming pool and the polio far behind you.

The soles of my feet felt hot from the friction but however hard I pushed down on my skates, however hard I pushed on, I was never able to build up much of a head of steam.

However, here I was, a lifetime later, feeling absurdly pleased with myself, pleased with the very idea of my physio taking a celebratory photo of me. That's me, believe it or not, heroically balanced on her skateboard. But I was also aware (as I handed back her mobile) that Clare seemed, I don't know, a bit detached, possibly a little unhappy, anyway less her buoyant self.

It's all too easy to take strong, steady people for granted.

★

Rhossili

To return for a moment to youthful Swansea. I know it's difficult talking to someone about a book or a story if you haven't both read it, you have no common ground, but let's just for once risk it. Let's say you ask me which stories from *Portrait of an Artist as a Young Dog* stand out, which ones leap off the page: well, I would pick *Extraordinary Little Cough* and *Who Do You Wish Was With Us*? Both are set around Rhossili, a long and famous beach on the Gower peninsula, all of four miles, a beach I know well.

Extraordinary Little Cough is a brutally accurate story, painfully so if you have spent your life as a classroom teacher. It is a story to make you wince about bullying, one of the hardest things in a school to catch or to stop, in this instance bullying on a camping trip – the bullied boy is told he can't bat and he can't bowl and he can't make water. He can't even piss. And what is his nickname? Extraordinary Little Cough.

Can't bear it, I honestly can't. It's that good.

I would prefer, if I may, to focus on *Who Do You Wish Was With Us?*

In this story, Dylan Thomas, all five foot five and eight stone of him, and his friend Raymond Price (ten years older) set out on foot from the Swansea suburbs for the Worm's Head and Rhossili. That's a good walk, all of fifteen miles, but of course no distance at all to you, Clare. To you fifteen miles is peanuts.

Their loose-limbed strides take Dylan and Ray speedily along Sketty Road, faster than me on roller skates, swishing their sticks, walking with pride and mischief, quick pretenders with a sensual strut, their haversacks jumping on their backs. Ray smokes a pipe. When he re-lights it he cups his hands as if he's in a gale. As the mown lawns drop away behind them, they cross the common and go through the wood, the bushes brimming with birdsong, or have I said that before, yes I have, well spotted, two marks, it's one of Dylan's phrases, and they banter with some cyclists who ride past, a girl on a tandem shouting 'There's room for one behind, sonny boy'.

The atmosphere is jaunty and spirited and spiced with occasional put-downs. The detail and the mood are perfectly observed. Dylan, as green and carefree as he is in *Fern Hill*, feels he has 'more love in me than I could ever want or use'. Unaccustomed to happiness himself, Ray winks and says 'A couple of wild wanderers in Wales. God, I like this.'

Humming along, they walk five miles, which is a third of the way there, pulling blades of grass and talking like men and smoking hard to keep the gnats away, when the Rhossili double-decker comes along the lane and they get on and eat their lunch on board, boiled eggs and meat paste and they take it in turns to drink from the Thermos. They overtake the cyclists crawling up the hill and cheer at them. The pert girl on the tandem is now a straggler. Dylan suggests that when they get back they don't admit that they took the bus. 'Pretend we walked all day.'

When they arrive at Worm's Head they lark around and pose and posture and cross with springy steps the slippery stones. They laugh triumphantly as they look at the golden beach stretching away, why don't we live here all the time, and they point things out to each other, as though the other person was blind.

And then, for no particular reason, as sometimes happens on a long sunny day, the two of them have a brief quarrel.

'You think you're a country boy, you don't know a cow from a horse.' In no time at all, Dylan can tell what is going to happen next because he knows Ray. He can read him, read him like the back of his hand. He can tell by his body language, the way Ray lowers his head and stares at his dusty shoes. He knows only too well what Ray is seeing and what shapes his imagination is making of those sights.

For Ray has lost his family, and it's all going to come out all over again. His father and sister and brother are dead. His mother, crippled with arthritis, is in a wheelchair. Withdrawn now from his day out with Dylan at Rhossili, Ray is pitched back into those ghastly bedrooms, carrying basins, listening for hand bells, and changing the sheets with blood on everything. He is holding down his father on the bed when he has his fits. 'Father thought I was trying to murder him. And when he died, he rattled.'

But even more than his father, Ray is thinking of Harry, his brother, who wasted away, his hands and his legs thinning before his eyes. Is it polio? This is the image Ray cannot shake off. 'Ray, look at my legs. Are they thinner today?'

Dylan briskly sympathises but tries to jolly Ray out of his mood, talking nineteen to the dozen, coming up with anything to head off the gloom. Then, led by Dylan, Ray climbs down to the sea and he is back in the open world perched on an overhang as he dangles his feet in the water. One of his shoes slips off. They fish it out. 'Never mind,' Ray says, 'it is worth it. I can't tell you how much I enjoyed it.'

The day and the rock and the world are theirs, as they were to be in my future and in my past for my friends Michael and Blondie and me, until Dylan asks Ray, 'Who do you wish was with us?' and before Ray can answer the question Dylan comes up with a couple of names himself, 'well, there's George and there's Gwilym, but who do you wish was with us, Ray?'
'I wish my brother was with us,' Ray said. 'I wish Harry was here. I wish he was here now, at this moment, on this rock.'

The sun goes down, the chill creeps up and the sea comes in. They are nearly cut off by the tide. Running back in the fading light they just make it. The slippy stepping stones are gone and the waves quickly cover the flat-backed rocks where they sat and dried their feet, the rocks covered with friends, living and dead.

I do not think this perfect little story is self-indulgent, and if it is considered to be so then count me guilty. It moves me more than anything Kingsley Amis, for all his wonderfully comic set pieces, ever wrote. It was warm and true when Dylan Thomas wrote it in the late 1930s. It was warm and true when my friends Michael and Blondie and I were there in the 1950s. Ten years later, I read the story out loud to one of my classes, doing the Welsh accents in a rather stagey voice, doing my passably over the top take-off of an already overblown Richard Burton.

Or Emlyn Williams

Or Philip Madoc

Or, as it now would be, Rob Brydon.

★

In 1936, with Stalin purging millions and Hitler on the march, Dylan Thomas published this poem on the consequences of unbridled individual power. He chose not to set it in his own time. Great terror is timeless.

> The hand that signed the paper felled a city;
> Five sovereign fingers taxed the breath,
> Doubled the globe of dead and halved a country;
> These five kings did a king to death.
>
> The mighty hand leads to a sloping shoulder,
> The finger joints are cramped with chalk;
> A goose's quill has put an end to murder
> That put an end to talk.
>
> The hand that signed the treaty bred a fever,
> And famine grew, and locusts came;
> Great is the hand that holds dominion over
> Man by a scribbled name.
>
> The five kings count the dead but do not soften
> The crusted wound nor stroke the brow;
> A hand rules pity as a hand rules heaven;
> Hands have no tears to flow.

Dylan Thomas was twenty-two when he wrote that.

★

Throw your scarf as high as you can above your head and catch it on the way down. We call this the scarf snatch.

★

Wilfred and Eileen

In a sense, two of my novels – *Wilfred and Eileen* (1976) and *Summer in February* (1995) – were 'given' to me. Both those books came directly from conversations I had as an English teacher, one with a pupil, one with a colleague. Both are what is loosely called 'true stories', and both are set in 1913 and 1914. When I told my mother how they had come about she smiled and said, 'Ah, so those stories landed in your lap, Jonathan.'

I came across the lives of Wilfred and Eileen in a rather roundabout fashion. In the early 1970s I was hoping to write something on Siegfried Sassoon, either a biography or a critical introduction of some kind. To be honest, I didn't mind what kind of book it was as long as it was published. And I intended concentrating not so much on Sassoon's war poetry, which was already widely known, if not becoming obligatory in the classroom, but more on his undervalued prose and in particular on the semi-autobiographical *Complete Memoirs of George Sherston*. I have always greatly admired that self-effacing trilogy.

The first of the three books, *Memoirs of a Fox Hunting Man*, is located in and around the Weald of Kent, where I live, and although the place names have been changed it isn't difficult to spot Tonbridge, Paddock Wood, Sevenoaks, Matfield and so on. The central character and narrator, George Sherston, is of course Sassoon's *alter ego*. The setting is an upper middle class world of farm carts and slow trains and point-to-points and village cricket. It has a nostalgic feel. The second (and most famous) volume of the trilogy, *Memoirs of an Infantry Officer*, pitchforks George Sherston and the reader from the serene innocence, if not complacence, of that country house rural England straight into the trenches. It is, of course, one of the great books of The Great War.

So, one morning, when I was teaching some poems by Isaac Rosenberg, my mind was also on Sassoon's journey from the

Flower Show Cricket Match to the Somme to Craiglockhart Hospital. After the lesson I found one of my pupils, a very able one, Anthony Seldon, waiting for me outside my classroom door. 'It's just that ...' he said, speaking very quietly, very privately, 'it's just that something really extraordinary happened to my grandparents. Back in the First World War. I didn't want to mention it in class, but I've been thinking you might like to know.'

'I would. Tell me more.'

And he did. He told me the story of Wilfred and Eileen, only the barest of outlines, in a chat that probably lasted no more than five minutes. That was the conversation, however, which started me out as a writer. That was my lucky break.

Anthony explained that his mother, Marjorie Seldon, had considerable autobiographical material left by her father, Wilfred Willett, and that Marjorie had tried unsuccessfully to find a publisher. Would I like to speak to her about it all, to find out more, and perhaps to read what his grandfather had written? Yes, I would. The very next weekend I drove over to their home near Sevenoaks, where Marjorie and her husband, Arthur Seldon, the distinguished economist, lived. Two hours later, encouraged to 'see what I could do with it', I was on my way back with Wilfred's battered manuscript beside me.

On one level, it was easy enough to understand why no publisher had yet been found. Much of it read as an unremarkable philosophical tract, tracing the path of Wilfred's political beliefs, but in the early part I could see a shattering and inspiring story. And, late one night, unable to sleep, I kept leafing backwards and forwards through the pages in that first short section. Then it happened. It is the moment when it all steals up on you and your hands tremble a little and your mouth goes dry and then your hands slowly drop down and you just sit there and stare straight ahead. I felt unwell. I was not quite all there. It was as if I was sickening for something. This is a sign which I have since come to recognise in myself, and to welcome. It means I am up and running.

Those pages of Wilfred's, I realised, had something of Siegfried Sassoon's simple directness and self-effacement, yet both men were not as simple or as self-effacing as they at first seemed. They were tough individuals. They'd had it good and they'd had it bad. Though different in so many ways, Siegfried and Wilfred were privileged and talented and trusting young men who had no inkling of what was to come. Both had been to famous public schools, Marlborough and St Paul's, and both were Cambridge graduates whose fortunate and promising lives seemed destined for the top. Then both had been traumatised by bullet wounds, after which each took up a political and moral position which set them sharply at odds with their own class.

And, of course, at the very heart of it all was a wonderful love story, that of Wilfred and Eileen.

Moving on, how on earth did Wilfred ever come to accept that his career as a surgeon had been blown away? All right, he had no choice. How did he endure his life-long disability and stay so positive and become so helpful, day in and day out, to so many others? I was hooked by Wilfred's astonishing courage and idealism. As for Eileen: how on earth did she overcome every obstacle and get to France on her own and bring him back home? How could a woman of her conventional background be so assertive and tenacious and strong? I was hooked by her extraordinary determination. In her refusal to be beaten she was in every way the equal of Wilfred. And who could not be deeply touched by their passion, their secret marriage and their total devotion to each other?

The facts were there. It is, however, a tricky thing lifting out a section of a real person's life and trying to turn it into a novel. When writing fiction or drama about real people in the past, the further back in time you go the easier it is. You can write just about anything you like about the Romans and the Elizabethans, and they do. It is much trickier, though, if the direct descendants, the close family, are still living. A father's real life or a mother's real life is more than a 'story' to a living son or a living daughter; it's far more important and far more potentially touchy than mere historical material to be shaped and re-written.

Marjorie Seldon, the most devoted of daughters, had entrusted me, then, not only with a manuscript but, in a way, with the private and intimate lives of her parents. Whatever I wrote, if it were published, would establish how Wilfred and Eileen were – from then on – to be known and to be remembered. From the first moment I set off on writing the book Marjorie was a massive help, open-hearted and open-minded, and in her own approach as determined as her parents in seeing something through. She backed me and she trusted me and she said so.

Yet, this always felt delicate territory. I was planning to transform a small part of a largely factual manuscript into a novel, and in this I knew I had to tread very carefully. While trying to make the story 'work', I needed to think hard about the issues of freedom and licence. I would have to use my imagination, you can't write a novel if you don't, but I should be wary of taking liberties. Where exactly should I play straight, and where could I reasonably embellish? Twenty years later I faced exactly these questions again when I was writing my fifth novel, *Summer in February*.

When you research an historical novel you spend months, years even, reading, taking notes, going to libraries, interviewing people, looking at old photographs and poring over diaries, revisiting places and taking new photographs. Then there are the quiet hours of sitting and waiting and staring and feeling: of being imaginatively with them. You can't get away with doing one or the other. Both approaches are essential and both take time.

I do like the physical part of the research. The notebooks, the maps, the tape recorder and the sharpened pencils, I enjoy all that. As a teaching colleague once put it to me, I have always been a bit of a failed historian. If you are going to write about real people, or if you are going to re-create (as far as you can) people who actually lived, the least you can do is put in the leg work. And there is in most writers something of the detective, something of the secret agent with a touch of the subversive mindset. I confess that I like being on the case. It is invigorating being on the scent, being a stalker of the past, keeping myself to myself but stealing up on something from an oblique angle, imagining I am in another world and playing the role of another man or (more difficult for me) a woman.

When I am doing all this I also try to let things happen and unfold, to be as much like blotting paper as I can be; I try to leave myself open to surprises and to random events. I try not to push. Yes, in my determination to 'get things right' I have travelled in a planned and purposeful spirit to many places, at home and abroad, but I also allow myself the time and space to wander, emotionally and physically, and that has often been rewarded.

My first (and easiest) *Wilfred and Eileen* visit was to Cambridge, which I know well. Wilfred was at Trinity College; fifty years later I was at the college next door, St John's. There was a nice moment in the Trinity Library when I held in my hand the menu for supper at the May Ball, 1913, the very meal that Wilfred and Eileen tasted on the day they first met each other. Were undergraduates much the same then? Were they very like me and my 1960s friends? Yes, no, yes and no, who knows.

Then I visited hospitals in London. I spoke to doctors and surgeons and medical historians. True, I had less luck finding the army camp in Crowborough where Wilfred trained with the London Rifle Brigade before being sent to the Front, but it did lead me into a good long walk in Ashdown Forest.

Years later, just after dawn one misty morning, I set off from Ypres with Wilfred's grandson, Anthony Seldon, for Ploegsteert

Wood, where Wilfred was shot in the head. It is difficult to be sure now of the exact spot, to be confident we were on the very same patch of ground over which he ran to help a wounded man – only to be hit himself. But we were there or thereabouts, we were close, we knew that, and we retraced our steps quietly back to the car.

Sooner or later there comes the moment, of course, when you have to put all this research aside, or behind you, and jump. You have to pick up your pencil and write. If you can't do that you should be writing a pamphlet not a novel. You have to trust that you know enough, that you've done the necessary preparation, and now it is about hooking the reader. Now it is not only about the demands of the narrative, it is about capturing states of mind and states of feeling. You have – if you are me – to fall in love with the characters (and then fall out of love with them before you can write your next book). You have to keep sharpening the dialogue. You have to strike the big moments hard, but not over-hit. You have to write as movingly as you can, which in my case means that I should under-write. You should, above all, treat the reader as a highly intelligent and perceptive person, who can join up the dots. You may need, as you go into the story, to hold the reader's hand lightly for a short while but then you must let go. You should push the story halfway across the table and hope the readers will reach out and pull it over to their side.

As a writer of historical fiction – broadly speaking, half of my novels and half of my plays have been set in the past – you are often asked, sometimes aggressively, sometimes with real animus, 'So, it isn't all true then? You made some of it up. Which bits did you make up? Bit of a cheek, isn't it? Taking a bit of a liberty, aren't you?' But then I've already interrogated myself with all those questions and have come to terms with what I will or will not defend. And, as the years go by, I admit I am finding it harder and harder to remember where and when the research stopped and where the imagination took over.

Anyway, by November 1973, just before I flew off with my wife and baby daughter to teach in Australia, I had finished a draft of *Wilfred and Eileen*. But was the novel, was my 're-creation' of that momentous episode in Wilfred and Eileen's lives, any good? Was it worth sending to anyone? Well, I knew one thing. I wanted it to be read by someone *serious*, someone I didn't know, someone who would be direct with me rather than kind and sensitive to my feelings. I needed, if you'll forgive the First World War metaphor, to put my head above the parapet. The trouble was I didn't know 'anyone'. I had no contacts in the literary or publishing world. So I scoured my bookshelves and stopped in my tracks and nodded to myself and did the unforgivable. I sent the manuscript to a writer I admired but had never met. This is a cheek and no mistake. It is an infuriating thing to do to most writers, even if you know them, as if they haven't more than enough on their own plates.

I sent it to Margaret Drabble, whose novels I greatly enjoyed. She was an intellectual, too, and happily unafraid of being seen to be so; she had a sharp eye and her finger was on the pulse of the everyday. She was also an outstanding literary critic who clearly had a first class mind. Right, so she wrote bestselling novels, she had babies, she lived a demanding life, she did it all, plus she had published a wonderfully lucid critical study of my favourite writer, Wordsworth, so she surely had enough time on her hands to read a draft of a first novel sent to her by some random English teacher in Kent?

Weeks passed. Well, what did I expect? There was no reply from Margaret Drabble. After a while I gave up checking the post. The only words I heard came from my conscience and my conscience was very direct: your letter has been ignored, you've been binned and quite right too, you've got your just deserts, it's a condign punishment, and you should be embarrassed by your pushiness. Never ever do that again. It's crass.

Then, on the morning my father was about to drive us to Heathrow, with us all gathering at the front door, with our cases packed and ready to go, the postman called, his last delivery before we left England. There was a letter from Margaret Drabble. I can see her handwriting now, as large as mine is small. No, she didn't normally read unsolicited manuscripts, but she liked my book. In fact she liked it a lot.

Oh, I *flew* to Australia all right.

Fly me to the moon, Frank Sinatra.

In 1975, on my return from Melbourne, I was made even happier. Philippa Harrison, then an editor at Hutchinson, said that she wanted to publish it. She was as good as her word, and she remained my publisher for almost thirty years. Philippa stuck by me through thick and thin, and my debt to her is incalculable. *Wilfred and Eileen* was well-received in the literary pages in 1976. The novel was dramatised on Radio 4 in 1983 and then serialised on BBC TV in four parts in 1984. Eight million people watched it.

Over the years since this, my first novel, came out I have come to see the story rather differently. When I wrote it I was in my early thirties and I identified with Wilfred, the bold young doctor who was going to change the face of medicine and become a famous consultant, the young officer to whom the men looked up, the ambitious and confident young man with the hooded eyes who had married a beautiful girl against everyone's wishes. But I now see it more as Eileen's story. My mind is more with her, and not only in the war years.

From 1916 to 1961 Eileen 'ran' their life together in The Rosery, their small Georgian house in Matfield. In the 'peaceful years' of the 1920s she saw Wilfred through his depressions. Later she helped him through the frustrations of his surgical boot and the irons which were intended to take some of the strain off his paralysed leg. She took visitors out to see Wilfred as he sat writing or watching birds in his hut. She drove her disabled husband everywhere in her car, everywhere he needed to go, to Maidstone and beyond, all over Kent, to this National Union of Agricultural Workers Union meeting, to that role in the War Pensions Welfare Service, as he pursued the political vision she did not share. She helped him to make the very best use he could of the life she had saved for him.

Throughout the 1930s Wilfred, now a committed communist, sold the *Daily Worker*, standing at his selling spot in Camden Road, Tunbridge Wells. Lenin, the Revolution and Tunbridge Wells. Eileen was only grateful it wasn't Matfield. I can't imagine Wilfred sold many copies. Not that he would have been daunted one little bit as that left even more people to be converted. No doubt some thought him potty or a crank, another man mentally damaged by his war wounds. He was, in fact, an English eccentric of a certain kind, an idealist with a hint of fanaticism.

He was also the sweetest of men. One of Wilfred's most frequent visitors in Matfield was the young Richard Cobb, later to be Professor of History at Oxford, who wrote the following in 1985:

> Wilfred was one of the best people I have ever met; and he also had a wonderful gift of making me feel important, that what I did or thought mattered and would make a difference. After all these years, I still miss him as much as ever, just as I can still see him, with his beautiful, slightly lop-sided smile, his rather bulbous and kindly eyes smiling too, hear his patient, halting speech and welcoming voice, and marvel at his ability to cope with his physical disadvantages. He is still absolutely alive for me. He is one of those rare people who, just by being there, by being himself, has enriched my life and filled me with optimism about human nature.

Eileen devoted her life to Wilfred; Wilfred devoted his life to others. In the grounds of Tonbridge Castle there is a bench with a plaque which reads: 'Donated by Tonbridge Trades Council in memory of their secretary, Wilfred Willett.' When I was researching *Wilfred and Eileen* in the early 1970s I interviewed old trade unionists in the town who knew him well. Wilfred worked, they said, much harder and for much longer hours than able-bodied men. He made no concessions to his disability. 'And he was different from us. He could write really good letters.' One said to me, 'Wilfred tried to live out the Sermon on the Mount. No one has ever inspired me so much.'

I have written this in my garden hut. In fact, I am only a few miles from where Wilfred – in his corduroy trousers and old sports coat with leather patches – sat in his garden hut, smelling of wood-smoke, writing his weekly nature column for *The Daily Worker*. On the shelf beside me I have his book, *British Birds*. As well as medicine and politics, Wilfred knew a great deal about trees, badgers and foxes. He also published a book about flowers. And he liked opera. So Eileen, naturally, drove him up to Sadler's Wells.

After forty eight years of marriage, Wilfred and Eileen died within six weeks of each other in 1961. I would never have known about their extraordinary lives, let alone been able to write my first novel, without the help and encouragement of their daughter, Marjorie, and their grandson, Anthony Seldon, now Sir Anthony, who waited for a word with me outside my classroom door.

★

Death of a Salesman

Which reminds me:

When I was teaching in Australia one of the set texts was *Death of a Salesman*, and the English department there, as well as being full of fine teachers, was well equipped with audio recordings. On their shelves in the office they had the superb version of Arthur Miller's play with Lee J. Cobb as Willy Loman and a young Dustin Hoffman as Bernard. I knew of Lee J. Cobb, of course, from his role as Johnny Friendly, the gangland union boss in *On the Waterfront*, and also as Juror 3 against Henry Fonda's Juror 8 in *Twelve Angry Men*.

Two great performances, two great movies.

Each lesson – these were fifteen/sixteen year-old boys – we read *Death of a Salesman* around the class in the old-fashioned way, discussing it as we went along, and then we listened to the same section on the tape recording. If I could, as a bonus, I always liked to end the lesson with those American cadences still in their ears and the haunting sound of that flute lingering in the warm air of their imaginations. At the weekends I set some homework, I can't remember precisely what that was, and on Monday mornings I collected in their essays. In the evening I marked them. Near the bottom of the pile of essays one boy had written his one word response to the homework, and in case I missed it he had written it in big capitals: SHITHOUSE.

The next day I had a private word with him, what we teachers like to call a quiet word, explaining that he just couldn't do that. He said that was what the play was, exactly that. I had, he reminded me, asked them all for their honest views, and I had also urged them not 'to come up with some master-pleasing job' (he precisely echoed my words) and he said his honest view of *Death of a Salesman* was as printed. I should add, as it is relevant in this instance, that he was archetypically handsome. He was well built, he moved gracefully and he was very good looking: an Adonis.

I told him to do the work again and to do it properly this time. He said he couldn't and he wouldn't and I said oh yes you can and you will and he said he couldn't bear the whole thing in fact every time he opened the book it made him want to puke and I told him I thought it was a pretty special play and I was off on one of my why-Arthur-Miller-is-worth-studying homilies when his head dropped and he broke down. He sat there sobbing. He said that he didn't come to school for this, he couldn't take it and he wouldn't take it.

-Why is that?

-Because.

-Because?

-Because ... because it's Dad. It's Dad and me.

At that he stood up and hurried away.

Later, over a cup of tea in the staff room, I asked a couple of colleagues about him. They had plenty to say. He was an outstanding footballer whose father's lifelong ambition was to have his son play at the highest professional level of sport. The father spent the weekends driving him to watch football matches, then on to extra practice sessions, and early Sunday mornings meant fitness training down on the beach. The father was already in touch with a number of first class clubs and there was some talk of a contract. And the girls fancied him.

His father was Willy Loman; the boy was Biff Loman; and the family was a car crash.

The next lesson, and for the remainder of our class time on Arthur Miller's play, the boy sat quietly. He was no trouble. He didn't disrupt the discussions or glare at me or sulk. He just sat the whole thing out, wordless. It was only when we moved on to the next book, a collection of poems by Bruce Dawe, that he tuned back in. He responded to Bruce Dawe's work, as did many of the class. One day he asked me a question about an elusive line in the poem we were studying, and from then on we were more or less all right.

One Saturday I went to watch him play football. He was good. Much later in the year, in the way that sometimes happens after you have clashed badly with a pupil, he asked me if I would like to visit his family. Would I like to go over to his place one weekend? Did I like the beach? They lived near the beach. He'd like to show me his beach. I said I would like that, and I told him about my schoolboy beach in Wales, my Dylan Thomas beach, Rhosilli, on the Gower peninsula.

That scene in Melbourne was fifty years ago, and every now and then, a thousand and more pupils later, with many of them no more than figures in a fog, I see him still, the boy, and sometimes wonder how everything turned out.

★

If I was faced with a mildly anti-intellectual, pleasantly philistine, averagely anti-books class of sixteen year-olds, the kind of class who say, 'What, *all* of it?' when you ask them to read a novel, and if I was told that I could only use three writers in my attempt to win them round to a love of English literature, I would choose Shakespeare, Philip Larkin and Arthur Miller.

Sorry? Did I miss something?

Did you say Shakespeare, Larkin and Miller? Shakespeare? Well, given our cross-dressing days they might like boys playing girls playing boys, but they won't get much of the language, let alone the literary conventions. And Larkin? He's too gloomy and too depressing. Not so, not so, I retort, he's permanent and true. But what are the kids going to *relate* to, come on, Jonathan, the poems don't *resonate*, they've got a long life ahead of them unless Larkers persuades them to end it all early, and you need to lighten things up a bit. They always love a good musical. As for Miller, OK he was married to Marilyn Monroe for a while, which is a start, there are some absolutely great posters available on the internet, that one of her white skirt flying up and Marilyn not trying all that hard to keep it down, and you could always show them the video of *Some Like it Hot*, that's three lessons worth, possibly four, mind you, Arthur Miller's not English, he's American, so he doesn't count anyway.

Even so, I would stick to my guns. Shakespeare, Larkin, Miller. And I've just remembered something else, a nice line about literature by Elizabeth Bowen. *Literature,* Elizabeth Bowen wrote, *once one knows it, drains away some of the shockingness out of life.*

Bang on.

I would say that by reading Arthur Miller my pupils would learn more, grow up more, face up to more (especially the shockingness), think more deeply, feel more deeply, understand more fully what literature can do by studying Miller's plays than by studying any other English speaking playwright in the second half of the twentieth century.

Failures and defects being inseparable from humanity, we are all flawed. We all need to care, we all need some help, we all need to be afforded some dignity and to be offered some kind of redemption, and I believe – with Dr Johnson – that great literature is primarily moral and mirrors life. Great literature, in its most serious forms – for example Shakespeare's tragedies and histories – confronts us with men and women facing misfortunes in a manner that self-pitying memoirs and misery porn do not.

And going back to Larkin for a second, achieved art, as Martin Amis said, can never be depressing.

In exploring the extraordinary 'normalities of human nature' Miller's work is, then, primarily moral. It lasts and it hits home and it stands up to sustained analysis, whereas Tom Stoppard's plays, for all their wow factor and the dazzling pleasure they give me in the theatre, do not. There is, by the way, a fair bit of Dr Johnson woven into these paragraphs and here he is again:

> The irregular combinations of fanciful invention
> may delight awhile, by that novelty of which the
> common satiety of life sends us all in quest; but the
> pleasures of sudden wonder are soon exhausted, and
> the mind can only repose on the stability of truth.

Many of the tough personal questions and dilemmas we all have faced in our lives are explored in Miller's sharply crafted, fully rounded and powerful dramas. They have the stability of truth. I started to read him in 1960 in the University Library at Cambridge. I started to teach him in Scotland in 1964, and I rarely missed a year when I did not take a play of his into class with me. Quite often the atmosphere in the classroom while we read him was subdued and serious and inward and reflective and silently responsive, unlike the practice in many contemporary lessons when all the pressure is to say something even when there is nothing to be said.

Yes, Miller's works are 'well-made plays' (whatever weight that absurdly pejorative term still carries, a patronising dismissal that was also wrongly applied to Terence Rattigan); yes, they are formally indebted to classical Greek tragedy (excellent, what's wrong with that?); and yes they are clearly influenced by Ibsen (and who better?).

The family dynamic, the central nervous system of drama, is at the core of Arthur Miller's plays. Indeed all of us are a part (however loosely) of a family in one sense or another. And as family members we know at first hand about the thickness of blood and water. We may be lucky enough in our upbringing to be given unconditional love and yet still feel the bond too tightening. In any lifetime of a family we are also likely to witness lovelessness or strife or breakdown or spoiling or favouritism or the blame game or irresponsibility or everyday claustrophobia, not to mention the many and varied ways in which epic rows tend to kick off over the dinner table, in my childhood experience often starting mildly with 'It's on the table and going cold and I won't say it again.'

In any Arthur Miller play each person has his or her own story to tell. It may be self-promoting, self-sustaining, self-deluding or self-destructive. But it is *their* story. It may be blindly loving or idolising or cocksure or dangerously idealistic or dangerously cynical. But it is their story and they cling to it and they will fight, and if need be fight to the death, to keep it inviolate.

In any Miller play you may well encounter husbands v wives, fathers v sons, brother v brother, past v present, public v private, and every variation on those central conflicts. There are destructive affairs and sexual taboos, there's plenty of vengeance and destruction, frustrated passions, codes of honour, turning of blind eyes, overwhelming ambitions, the price we pay for success, different versions of the past, re-writing history, family myths and long-held grievances and the way the past can come back to haunt us with the iniquities of the fathers being visited upon their sons, yea, (see Exodus, Deuteronomy and Numbers) even until the third and fourth generation.

Apart from God dooming certain families, does any of that sound familiar?

Yes, it could be Greek tragedy.

Anyone else?

Yes, it could be Henrik Ibsen.

If you pressed me further to select which particular plays of Arthur Miller to study, I would go for *All My Sons, Death of a Salesman* and *The Price*. I could, I suppose, just as easily pick *The Crucible, A View from the Bridge* and *The Last Yankee*. Indeed a case could be made for any play of his. But the first three have a great deal in common – exploring the choices we make and the painful price we may pay for them, as we cover up our complicity and dread the day of reckoning – and they would work fruitfully and well together.

If the plays I selected all failed to grab the class, if the class talked among themselves or smirked or put their feet up on the desk or ate some chocolate or looked out of the window or kept on saying, 'Sor-*ry*, sir, but I just don't get it', I would take the early retirement package or, as it used to be called by my more cynical colleagues, the breakdown pension.

Ten years or more after the incident in my Melbourne classroom I saw the Dustin Hoffman film of *Death of a Salesman* in a London cinema. This time Dustin Hoffman was playing Willy Loman, the central character, and John Malkovich was his Adonis of a son, Biff, who let his father down, or whose father let him down. About a third of the way through I slowly became aware that a woman in the row behind me was weeping. She wept quietly throughout the film.

★

letting your father down

Shakespeare wasn't the only actor or writer to enjoy cross-dressing, who liked to play at – or indeed to become – the opposite sex. In many societies, of course, it's as old as the hills, and in England any number of late seventeenth and early eighteenth century playwrights indulged in the game, if a game it was. John Dryden, Thomas Shadwell, William Wycherley, Mrs Aphra Benn – the first English woman to earn her living by writing – and Colley Cibber all wrote roles for women who had to pass muster as men. These were known in the theatre as 'breeches parts', and the audiences took to them. They became the thing. They were the buzz. As well as affording pratfall potential, cross-dressing gave an extra edge to the action, a sense of risk, and of course there was always the excitement of unexplored sexual frisson.

Being a cross-dresser as an actor, treating someone as a girl who is a boy or being treated as the opposite sex yourself, is not unlike being a novelist. You are free, if you wish, to park your conventional, straight, sensible self. You may be any sex or both. There are no gender guidelines. You may switch. You choose. You may, if you wish, allow your unspoken desires to be fulfilled and your too censored imagination to run loose. As a writer, you can do what you like and be who you like, and as you do so you can feel the power and the surge in your veins. It's heady.

> You are a creator.
> You can be God, The Creator.
> Or even a humble fly on the wall.
> Or all of the above.

It's not just a matter of males wearing make-up, it gives, for example, females the chance in every sense to wear the trousers. You can pull on or take off any clothes, it's up to you how many masks you wear or how many shoes you step into, from baby shoes to stilettos to your last scuffed slippers, it's up to you how you dress or undress or are addressed.

No one has cross-dressed more wholeheartedly, or for longer spells, than Charlotte Charke (1713-1760). I discovered her, appropriately enough, while browsing in a bookshop in Kemptown, Brighton. (Brecon in the 1950s and Brighton in the 2020s are far more than seventy years apart and far more than two hundred and fifty miles away. Brighton in 2020 was simply unimaginable in Brecon in the 1950s.)

The book I came across, or had pointed out to me, in that Brighton bookshop was *The Well-Known Trouble Maker: A Life* by Charlotte Charke and Fidelis Morgan. Charlotte was the eleventh and youngest child of Colley Cibber. Colley Cibber was an actor-manager and a playwright as well as an adapter of other dramas (e.g. when he wasn't re-writing Shakespeare's comedies he was crucifying Molière). He was also the Poet Laureate in 1730 (don't ask me how) and the hero of Pope's mock-heroic *The Dunciad*. Colley Cibber was prolific, shallow, brash, vain and hugely successful: always a combination hard to swallow.

From her earliest days Charlotte was determined to follow in her famous father's footsteps. She, too, wanted to be an actor, to be a playwright and a success. Indeed, from the first steps she took Charlotte was a performer to her fingertips. At four she was discovered walking up and down in a ditch outside the family home, dressed from top to toe in male clothes. She had big boots on, her brother's waistcoat, her father's wig, her father's large beaver hat and, to round it off, behind her she was dragging a large sword. A crowd gathered to watch and to applaud the strutting girl. She bowed with a low flourish to each passer-by. As she swaggered up and down the ditch, everyone was captivated by the sight except the one person Charlotte was above all keen to impress: her father. He was appalled. From that day on Colley Cibber considered her unnatural, a cause of family shame, and quite simply a disgrace.

This early rift was never healed. Not even partly. Throughout her adult life, and in her book, Charlotte asked to be forgiven (for what I have never been sure) but forgiven she never was. On her helter-skelter picaresque journey back and forth across England she impressed many people in the theatrical and literary world but when he died Colley Cibber left his thousands to other relatives and '£5 and no more' to Charlotte.

Charlotte was always in an extraordinary hurry. She was a hyper-active gypsy actress looking for work, always moving on, driven by a shortage of cash and by whatever else drove her, running towards or away from something. From Drury Lane or Covent Garden or the Haymarket Theatre to Bristol and Bath and Tunbridge Wells she was either on a stage or facing the hazards of the road. She played every role she could, male and female. Perhaps she was a Viola and a Rosalind and a Portia, the record is not clear, but she certainly played the foppish Roderigo in Othello, as well as Falstaff and the loud-mouthed Pistol in Shakespeare's history plays before taking on Macheath in Gay's The Beggar's Opera.

As a strolling player on the open road she always travelled as a Mr Brown in the company of a Mrs Brown. If she needed money, which she nearly always did, she took whatever job she could find to stay above the breadline. She became a gardener, a puppeteer, a waiter, a grocer, a pastry cook, a prompter and a proofreader. With her Protean gifts she could do anything and play anyone and be anyone. Work and play were to her the same thing:

> We players are a set of merry undone dogs, and though we often want the means of life we are seldom without the means of mirth. We are philosophers and laugh at misfortune; even the ridiculous situations we are sometimes placed in are more generally the cause of mirth than misery.

I do not know whether Charlotte Charke was heterosexual or bisexual or lesbian or trans. Or or. She was married twice and had a daughter. Those are facts which may or may not betoken something. I do not know whether she simply enjoyed being a provocative tomboy or was a deeply complex woman or bounced between many possibilities. It is plausible that she woke up each morning feeling she was, or would like to be, a different person. I do know she was a remarkable actress and a remarkably philosophical woman who could pass in real life as well as on stage for a man.

Far from being a vagabond or a deviant or a queer – all terms applied to her since her death – she was an entertainer, a trouper and a star. For her, life was uphill, up-hill all the way, yes, to the very end, as it is for some people, but despite her dreadful father she dusted herself off, stripped back the layers, dressed herself up and started all over again. With her cocked hat she endured. She died at forty-seven. In all things contradictory, Charlotte Charke was a natural, true to herself, or true to her many selves, and I would give anything to have her walk through that door.

Does the road wind up-hill all the way?
  Yes, to the very end.
Will the day's journey take the whole long day?
  From morn to night, my friend.

But is there for the night a resting-place?
  A roof for when the dark hours begin.
May not the darkness hide it from my face?
  You cannot miss that inn.

Shall I meet other wayfarers at night?
  Those who have gone before.
Then must I knock, or call when just in sight?
  They will not keep you standing at that door.

Shall I find comfort, travel-sore and weak?
  Of labour you shall find the sum.
Will there be beds for me and all who seek?
  Yea, beds for all who come.

Christina Rossetti (1830-1894)

★

the plinth

–How did you get on with the scarf snatch?

–Too easy. Kids stuff. Ask me another.

–Really? I'll check up on all that later. Right. Hug your right knee, lift it up, that's it, closer to your chest. Now your left knee. Now, locking your hands together, if you can, hug both your knees to your chest, and rock gently from side to side. I'll make sure you don't roll off.

–My left knee is hurting.

–Badly?

–No, creaking a bit.

-To do any good you have to go to the ouch level.

-O.K.

-But don't push it hard, ease it there.

I slowly got into it, and soon I was gently rocking, to the left, to the right, to my left, to my right, fractionally further each time, enjoying the feeling of easing and unlocking spreading along my lower back. I closed my eyes and, after a while, went with it. Into a kind of peace.

Imagine a mountain, with snow, and a train curving on a long bend. I gave in to the beat of a train, to the sway of a train, and the train I was on was bound, no surprises here, for Florence and I was going there with E.M. Forster. It was our birthday, a New Year's Day birthday treat to each other. I owe him a lot. I paid for his ticket. He taught me, I always carried him around in my undergraduate pocket, two cheers for democracy, and years later I was teaching at his school, and this time around I taught him. At the same moment, Clare was climbing Everest, in the distance but clearly nearing the summit, there she is, look, getting smaller step by small step all the way with Hillary and Tensing, 1953, the first woman to do so.

-What's making you smile?

-Nothing.

-No, go on. Don't be mean.

-No, it's nothing.

★

Saw the doctor. She says I may soon need to up my medication a notch or two, and that means I will need to up my exercise regime, just when my energy levels seem to be at a new low. And x-rays show my stoop is also more pronounced.

On the High Street, leaving the surgery, I caught sight of myself in a shop window. No. Can't be.

Which reminds me: driving in the South of France a while back I stopped at a petrol station to go to the loo. Walking towards the entrance to the lavatory I stepped aside, minding my manners, I always try to do that, giving way to let this old guy coming out go first. The old guy stepped aside in exactly the same way. I smiled and nodded and stepped the other way in this nicely timed after you, Claude, no, after you, Cecil comic routine. As did he.

I was facing a full length mirror.

★

Clare and I did a high five today. Led by her, of course. Still, it's a first for me.

★

E.M.F

On January 1st 1904 – and New Year's Day was his birthday, as it happens to be mine – E.M.Forster made some New Year Resolutions, as we tend to do. Whether he kept them on this occasion in 1904 I do not know. On January 1st 1904 Morgan Forster was 25, and on the edge of a period of astonishing creativity. Here are his resolutions:

One. Get up earlier.

Two. Smoke in public. It gives a reason for you, and you can observe unchallenged.

Three. Plan out work.

Four. More exercise, to keep the brutes quiet.

Five. Don't ever shrink from self-analysis, but don't keep on at it too long.

Six. Get a less superficial idea of women.

Seven. Don't be so afraid of going into strange places or company.

Eight. Be a fool more frequently.

Nine. Keep accounts.

On that same day, his twenty-fifth birthday, he also inherited £8,000, a considerable sum, and one which will have been as welcome to him as the similar inheritance which allowed the young Wordsworth, a hundred years earlier, the freedom to write *The Prelude*.

'I've made two great discoveries,' Forster added to his New Year Resolutions, 'the religious about four years ago, and the other in 1902.' By the 'religious' one he meant that he had abandoned Christianity, or at least the spiritual shallows that he knew, for truth and beauty and personal relations.

By the 'other one' he meant the nature of his sexuality, an area touched on from another angle in resolution four, 'more exercise, to keep the brutes quiet'. That is the old-fashioned exercise and cold shower option for males when faced with embarrassingly frequent and very visual arousal. But by 'the other' one Forster was acknowledging to himself, though he could not to the world, that he was homosexual.

Over the next three years Forster wrote, in an unusual overlapping way, his three early novels: *Where Angels Fear To Tread*, published in 1905; *The Longest Journey*, in 1907; and in 1908 *A Room With A View*. Three novels in three years, and still short of his thirtieth birthday.

By the way, I have always been somewhat slow at realising that this or that writer was homosexual, or indeed this or that friend. It wasn't, for example, until the early 1960s that it dawned on me that Christopher Isherwood was, and the early 1970s Siegfried Sassoon, and all this despite the fact that I had read and loved most of their work: a naïvety hard to believe, particularly with Isherwood – blimey, all those boys in Berlin, Jonathan, where have you *been*? – but it's true. Not that it matters that much.

Most readers, of any sexual persuasion, certainly most academic students of Forster, probably rate as his highest achievements his later works, *Howard's End*, 1910 and *A Passage to India*, in 1924, though the Merchant Ivory films have brought the early novels to a huge audience, as well as helping many A-level candidates achieve high grades without the hassle of actually reading the books. Mind you, the video substitute does have its dangers, especially if you risk believing in one of Andrew Davies's adaptations. I'm thinking of his version of *A Room With A View*, Forster's sunniest novel, which ends – in the adapter's version that is – with George Emerson dead in the First World War, though that conflict was still six years in the future.

Why on earth would you do that?

There are enough miserable moments in life already, and enough tragedies in literature, and certainly more than enough deaths in Forster's work, without adding to the toll. At the end of Forster's novel Lucy Honeychurch and George are happy lovers in a hotel room in Florence, enwrapped in youth and each other's arms. Andrew Davies has Lucy returning to her hotel room, and George is, yes, flat on his back all right but in a trench in Flanders.

E.M.F's least admired novel, his least read, and his most autobiographical book is *The Longest Journey*, which is partly based on Tonbridge School in Kent where I taught English for most of my career. Although published after *Where Angels Fear To Tread* he started writing it before.

How did E.M.Forster come to be at school in Tonbridge in the mid 1890s? He wasn't a man of Kent or a Kentish man or the son of a man in the City. And I'm not going to give you his family tree. To be frank, I can't be doing with biographies where you only get to the birth of the subject on about page 57 after you've flogged through his or her grandparents and parents and aunties and uncles.

So, very quickly:

Edward Morgan Forster was born in 1879, on New Year's Day you'll remember, at Clapham. He was an only child. His father, an architect who seems also to have had a homosexual nature, died before Morgan was two. After the metaphorical paternal lash, came the maternal embrace: E.M.F and his mother, Lily, moved from London to Stevenage in Hertfordshire. He went to a couple of schools, one of them a prep school in Eastbourne, when his mother suddenly moved to Tonbridge in 1893.

And the main reason for this decision was that her little outsider – small for his age, and no Adonis, as someone unkindly put it – her pallid, introspective, self-effacing boy, who walked in a slightly hunched way, could be a day boy at an academic school. He could live at home with her. If you lived within ten miles of Tonbridge parish church you could pay day boy fees, and the dayboy fees were attractive.

This is how Forster introduces Sawston/Tonbridge School in *The Longest Journey*:

> Sawston School had been founded by a tradesman in the seventeenth century. It was then a tiny town, and the City Company who governed it had to drive half a day through woods and heather on the occasion of their annual visit. In the twentieth century they still drove, but only from the railway station; and found themselves not in a tiny town, nor yet in a large one, but amongst innumerable residences, detached and semi-detached, which had gathered around the school. For the intentions of the founder had been altered, or at all events amplified, and instead of educating the 'poore of my home', he now educated the upper middle classes of England. The change had taken place not so very far back. Till the nineteenth century the grammar school was still composed of day scholars from the neighbourhood. Then two things happened.
>
> Firstly, the school's property rose in value, and it became rich. Secondly, for no obvious reason, it suddenly emitted a quantity of bishops. The

bishops, like the stars of a Roman candle, were of all colours, and flew in all directions, some high, some low, some to distant colonies, one into the Church of Rome. But many a father traced their course in the papers; many a mother wondered whether her son, if properly ignited, might not burn as bright; many a family moved to the place where living and education were so cheap, where day boys were not looked down upon, and where the orthodox and the up-to-date were said to be combined. The school doubled its numbers. It built new classrooms, laboratories, and a gymnasium. It dropped the prefix 'Grammar'. It coaxed the sons of local tradesmen into a new foundation, the 'Commercial School', built a couple of miles away. And it started boarding-houses. It had not the gracious antiquity of Eton or Winchester, nor, on the other hand, had it a conscious policy like Lancing, Wellington, and other purely modern foundations. Where traditions served, it clung to them. Where new departures seemed desirable, they were made. It aimed at producing the average Englishman, and, to a very great extent, succeeded.

Even though the passage is satirical, it also shows how deeply Forster had thought about his old school. He puts his sharply comic finger on a raw nerve, on something uncomfortably, if not devastatingly, close.

Morgan Forster was at Tonbridge School from 1893 to 1897, and he was the sort of boy over whom an over-worrying mother would worry. I can understand all of this as I was a bit of a mother's boy myself. I was a bit molly-coddled and compliant, a bit smothered, so I can sympathise. I can see Lily Forster worrying if her one and only dearest boy was wearing his vest, and was it warm enough when he put it on, and then worrying about his boiled egg, had it been runny enough for him or might the silly little goose get indigestion.

And just imagine how it would be these days. Morgan is about to cross the busy A26, the London Road, when his mobile rings and he fumbles for it and drops it and picks it up.

-Is that you, Morgan?

-Yes, Mother.

-Why did it take you so long to answer?

-My fingers were cold.

-Have you crossed the London Road yet, you little goose?

-No, Mother.

-Well, be careful, darling.

-I will, Mother.

-Has anyone been beastly to you yet, Morgan?

-Not quite yet, Mother.

-Well, the moment any of those rugby players come near you, dear, you run away and I'll get straight on to your housemaster.

-Would that be wise, Mother?

On his way down the school avenue, putting a few more yards between himself and Lily, between school and the sanctuary of home, a home where there was little vigour and little action beyond watching the tadpoles and where one was always urged to be careful, but now he was on his dangerous way towards raucous bustle and towards lessons, lessons in which he was to shine in a quiet, modest way. Morgan might have looked right at the cricket pitch or he might have looked left at the school buildings, but I suspect he kept his head down.

To give it further edge, the title of the novel comes from Shelley's *Epipsychidion* and refers to the nature of the marital relationship. It asserts the limitations of monogamy, of what we lose by only having one partner in life's long journey. When the young Forster first read the passage in Shelley he wrote in the margin, as clever young people tend to do, 'very good'.

I never was attached to that great sect
Whose doctrine is that each one should select
Out of the world a mistress or a friend,
And all the rest, though fair and wise, commend
To cold oblivion – though it is the code
Of modern morals, and the beaten road
Which those poor slaves with weary footsteps
    tread
Who travel to their home among the dead
By the broad highway of the world – and so
With one chained friend, perhaps a jealous foe,
The dreariest and the longest journey go.

Shelley (1792-1822)

The dreariest and the longest journey: a tough line and a tough title for a novel which is uneven in tone, a book that is comic and savage and warm and strange, a novel in which you could argue Forster took revenge on his old school. Almost half of the characters in *The Longest Journey* die, usually suddenly, and many of them mid sentence. If I were to find myself a character in an E.M.Forster novel I would be quite anxious about an approaching comma and if a semi-colon was coming round the corner, I'd be hyper-ventilating.

Schools have, of course, often been the setting for a good story, particularly for a satire. From *Tom Brown's Schooldays*, Thomas Hughes' 1857 novel set in Rugby, *To Serve Them All My Days*, R.F. Delderfield's public school saga, based I think on West Buckland School in Devon. From Dickens's Mr Gradgrind and from Dickens's Wackford Squeers, what a name for a schoolmaster, the headmaster of Dotheboys Hall in *Nicholas Nickleby*, to Zoe Heller's *Notes on a Scandal,* her 2003 novel and movie, not to mention *If* ... Lindsay Anderson's 1967 fine film set in a public school (and written by two Old Tonbridgians), to Alan Bennett's *The History Boys*, in which it was, on one level, gratifying to see that grammar school boys up north will cheerfully get up to things that have too long been supposed to be the exclusive territory of southern softies.

Sawston is, then, based on his time at Tonbridge School, a time in which he was, it is often repeated and even more often assumed, unhappy. Whatever people think Forster said about his schooldays, what did he actually say? This:

> Sawston owes something to my own public school. I was neither very happy nor very unhappy there, a Varden who never got his ears pulled. (Varden was a bullied boy in *The Longest Journey*.) The best of my life began when I left school, and I am always puzzled when other elderly men reminisce over their respective public schools so excitedly and compare them as if they were works of art: it sounds as if they must have had a dullish time since.

Those words, though, *was neither very happy nor very unhappy there,* are apt enough to describe my own schooldays, and perhaps those of many others. As a boy that was me: I was not obviously bullied though others were, and the best of my life began when I went to Cambridge, where, like Forster, I lost my faith, but, unlike Forster, did discover girls.

Perhaps I could, like Van Morrison, just open this up a bit and ask you the question? How happy were your schooldays? Happy? Good, that's great. So-so? I know what you mean. Unhappy? Tell me. And, while you are, what about all the boys and girls who have escaped the public school life, all those I see on the school buses as I walk to buy my paper each morning? What about them, those boys and girls? Are they happy/unhappy in normal measures? I can't tell. The bus driver always looks unhappy though.

But, anyway, would it be so odd if Forster was unhappy? Susceptible, creative people are eight to ten times more likely to suffer depression and mental illness. Alice Flaherty, the neurosurgeon, in her book *The Midnight Disease*, makes this clear. Amongst artists, painters, actors, writers, philosophers, and musicians the levels of anxiety and depression are disturbingly high, massively higher than amongst politicians, business people or scientists.

Hamlet had his problems, with his loss of enthusiasm, with his inability to take pleasure in life, a condition with which many of us are all too familiar. Writers often put down their problems to fatigue or to writer's block or to being undervalued, but it's not one of the Seven Deadly Sins to find the creative life difficult, to suffer severe mood swings, to recognise a loss of creative libido, a sense of diminishing testosterone. Stevie Smith puts this well in her little poem, *My Muse*:

> Why does my Muse only speak when she is
> unhappy?
> She does not. I only listen when I am unhappy.
> When I am happy I live and despise writing.
> For my Muse this cannot but be dispiriting.

But the comfort may be, in Leon Wieseltier's words, that if you can write about the wreckage then the wreckage is not complete. If you can keep writing there's a chance you're more or less intact. The despairing writer is never the most despairing person in the world. We write, in part, to prove that the wreckage is not complete.

So that private, quick-witted, non-games-playing pupil, who looks askance at you as you pass him in the corridor, what is he going through? His name might come up in a staff meeting. A teacher is worried and wants to see what other colleagues think. How distressed is the boy? Is there something we haven't been told? Is it a phase or is it big stuff? I've taught many creative, sensitive pupils. Were they bullied? Were their lives a misery? I hope not. But I don't know. Here is a passage from *The Longest Journey*, involving Rickie and Gerald, the games-playing bully.

> But Rickie and Gerald had met, as it were, behind the scenes, before our decorous drama opens, and there the elder boy had done things to him – absurd things, not worth chronicling separately. An apple pie bed is nothing; pinches, kicks, boxed ears, twisted arms, pulled hair, ghosts at night, inky books, befouled photographs, amount to very little by themselves. But let them be united and continuous and you have a hell that no grown-up devil can devise. Between Rickie and Gerald there lay a shadow that darkens life more often than we can suppose. The bully and his victim never quite forget their first relations.

That strikes me as a fine passage. It is fiction and, as with the best fiction, it rings more true than fact. Morgan Forster did not go through that; Rickie Elliot did. But you feel it, because Forster, with his acute empathy, felt it.

As a long-ago schoolboy and as a long-retired teacher that passage hits me hard. Forster is tough, very tough, and make no mistake. Gerald, the sporty bully, dies on a football pitch (on a pitch no doubt very like the ones on which, in all weathers, I coached cricket and rugby for many years). And Gerald doesn't just die. He is flicked off, rubbed out. The tone is disturbingly, if not comically cruel. It is the prose of condign punishment, the prose of a non-sporty schoolboy's revenge, served cold. Forster may not be a footballer but he knows how to put the boot in.

Before I leave E.M.F I want, though, and very tentatively, to suggest a slightly different reaction to schooldays unhappiness. (I am not, of course, talking here about extreme unhappiness, more what you might call normal unhappiness.) Is it not sometimes a rite of passage? And is it so wrong to say, even to admit, that some of the most insidious forms of bullying are almost impossible to defeat, for example an atmosphere of unkindness that no discipline can dispel?

Sometimes, too, may there not be a tendency to over-dramatise the ups and downs of one's schooldays? If it is a commonplace, as it is, for older men to lie repeatedly about their sporting achievements at school, may it not also be common for creative spirits and creative writers retrospectively to point up their unhappiness. To make the most artistic use of their victimhood?

I have no wish to glamourise teenage melancholia. Perhaps, though, it is the sense of exclusion, of not quite fitting in, of being different, of standing at an angle, a sense of being off the pitch, which sharpens the critical and creative faculty?

As a teacher I did what I could do when I sensed unhappiness, believing that the best pastoral care at my daily disposal was trying to come up with a good lesson, trying to amuse or stretch or lift especially those pupils who I felt might be feeling low, to imply by a look or an off-hand remark that I was on their side, rather than telling them that I felt their pain. I was a teacher and try as I might I was not a trained therapist with a one-to-one appointment book.

And a confession, albeit a bit late in the day: when I was a schoolboy in the 1950s I tended to embrace my boredom and to hug my unhappiness, if unhappiness is what it was. Was it all a bit of a game? I'm not sure, but for me being (or appearing to be) pissed off was probably my first professional role.

The years eleven to eighteen are unlikely to be easy, unless you fit hand in glove with your family and your school, and those that do rarely do much in later life. There's a lot of unresolved anger in teenage, and a lot of unresolved tension in creative people. They can have therapy, and that may well help, (and for me it certainly does, I have been in counselling for seven years now) but is there not, at the very least – and I put it no stronger – the risk that if you delete the doom and gloom, if you take away the demons, you take away the angels too?

So, we are back to where we started, to Forster's New Year Resolution number five:

'Don't ever shrink from self analysis but don't keep on at it too long.'

Forster is not straightforward. Few writers seem to be straightforward, not even the straight ones. He loved to play out and dramatise his hateful oppositions: England v India, England v Italy, Tunbridge Wells v Cambridge, the personal v the conventional, the spiritual v the social, the normal v the abnormal, the sensual v the intellectual.

The Longest Journey is his most difficult novel to grasp; it was, he surprisingly claimed, his favourite book, the one he was most glad to have written. And in it he struggled, as he always did, with love, liberty, beauty, affection and truth. In it, too, you can sense him, as Nicola Beauman says in her fine biography, beginning to lower the bucket into his subconscious, and bringing it up with that characteristic detachment. He's well on his way as a great writer, but though a stunning achievement for someone in his mid twenties, *The Longest Journey* is not, to my mind, a great book. It strikes me as patchy, uneven and brilliant, rich with promise, with Cambridge v Tunbridge Wells fought to the death, ending melodramatically on a distant Wiltshire railway line.

E.M.F is an elusive, tricky, equivocal writer. He's clever but he plays don't-let's-be-too-clever, which is a very English thing; he was an intellectual who claimed not to be able to think; a suburban who loathed suburbia, an Edwardian with much of the modernist mindset. He was timid but he loved to shock; he was sometimes open, sometimes closed, humble but cutting, a man who spent too much time in misogynist company but came to have many female friends, a man who hated bullies but could, when he wanted to, land blow after blow.

Katherine Mansfield was dismissive of Forster in a tone not dissimilar to the way in which some critical people dismiss Jane Austen. Mansfield said 'E.M.Forster never gets any further than warming the tea pot. He's a rare fine hand at that. Feel the teapot. Is it not beautifully warm? Yes, but there ain't going to be no tea.'

Wrong, wrong, wrong: she just missed it, she just didn't get it.

★

-Oh, yes, I knew there was something.

-Yes?

-Something I hadn't told you, Clare.

-I imagine there's quite a lot of that.

-The thing is I'm beefing up my team. I now have another therapist. This time it's speech and language. She's coming to my place to give me exercises.

-You decided you need that?

-Apparently my volume is down. So she says. My voice is softer, a bit whispery, a bit reedy. I have to say I've noticed people are leaning forward when I talk, straining to hear me, and looking a bit lost. And it's not just that they're all deaf.

-OK. What sort of things do you do with the new therapist? Breathing?

-Exactly, I have to take a deep breath. And then I say AAAH loudly, very loudly, holding my breath for as long as I can, maintaining my volume at a comfortable pitch. My record so far is fifteen seconds. When I started I was on a measly 9 seconds. Then I top up my breath, and repeat the exercise ten times. Then I do loud AAhs going up the scale on three notes, ten times, holding the highest note, then down the scale on three notes, holding the lowest note, ten times. D'you want to hear?

-Go for it.

-AAAAAAAAAAAAAAAAAAAaaaaaaaaaaaa. Sorry, tailed off a bit at the end.

-Wow.

-Then she asks me to list, as loudly as I can, all the ice cream flavours I can think of. Imagine Rowan Atkinson doing his list, pronouncing them very emphatically. Black-berry. But-ter-scotch. Chocolate Chip Cookie, Coff-ee. Tu-tti-Fru-tti. Fudge. Lem-on. Man-go. Pep-per-mint. Rum Raisin. Straw-berry. Toff-ee. Peach!

–Vanilla? You missed out vanilla.

–I was coming to that. But my favourite exercise so far, believe it or not, is listing all the towns in Kent.

–We should really be getting going.

–While maintaining a loud level throughout.

–Couldn't this, you know, wait for another time?

–Won't take a minute. Right. Towns in Kent. In alphabetical order. Ashford, Appledore, or is that a village, Bromley, Birchington, Broadstairs –

–When did you last get your meds checked?

★

PART TWO

I've read every word you sent me, Jonathan. How different we are. To me completing a book would be an epic adventure.

Your stories, or are they essays, come from reading books. Is that right? I am led by my hands and body. I suppose I am a doer. It runs in the family.

I was sixteen when I set off with my best friend from school on a cycling trip along the Loire, down the west coast of France. Just the two of us. My parents raised no objections. There was none of the 'are you mad, a girl at your age'. My idea of bliss then, at sixteen, was two weeks cycling or swimming or climbing. It still is.

Why do I step into freezing sea water on the south coast in only a swimming costume? My father was a sailor. My brother sailed round the world. So I decided to swim the English Channel, twenty-one miles. It was a challenge, the lure of a challenge. No big deal. Honestly. Or that is how we as a family approached it.

We met in the dark on the beach at Samphire Hoe, two miles from Dover. You may know of it.

I had a glow stick pinned to my back so that they could always see me in the water. My father came on the crossing boat, keeping his eye on the tides and currents, with his red oilskin peaked cap and his Guinness. Someone told me that two hundred and fifty women have swum the Channel before me, don't know if that's true, anyway fewer than have climbed Everest. It took me nineteen hours.

Some people find the sea a frightening place. I see it with a sense of freedom. I can go with the tide and the flow. I was always physically confident. I suppose I learnt to embrace adventure.

It was tough in the Channel, no point pretending otherwise, but I kept going. I loved seeing small boats and the tankers and the ferries, and then the French coast. When I landed a Frenchman gave me a heart shaped stone. I still have it. I said I would do a cartwheel when I got there but I fell in a heap.

That is about it.

I'll jot more things down as they come to me. I'm a bit nervous doing this, not confident at all. What they call out of my comfort zone. Writing isn't my thing. As I'm sure you can tell.

*

Jonathan, I'll add a bit more. Cycling. You asked me about cycling. I have a Red Raleigh racer with green Karrimor panniers with beige straps. The gears are on the frame not the handlebars. I don't have special shoes, just Adidas trainers.

We cyclists like to look good on our bikes, legs especially, and I'm one of them.

Gosh, just thinking about it, where haven't I been: Southern Spain, Pyrenees, coastal paths, I've trekked, climbed, cycled, in New Zealand, Norway, Canada, India, you name it.

Is all this any help? Am I boring you? You have a big interior life. Not sure I do.

Oh, and I did the Iron Man Outlaw thing in Nottingham. I broke my wrist eight weeks before, but I still did it on behalf of all my clients who are sort of broken too.

★

Thank you for all that. Samphire Hoe: I can see you setting off, Clare, on your swim from there. Samphire is an edible plant, isn't it, a bit like asparagus. You can sometimes buy it in the supermarket. Yes, you knew that. But the word *Samphire* rang a bell with me for other reasons. Of course it did, you know me,

I'm booky. Because we're back to *King Lear*.

Can I tell you why?

It's in *King Lear*, Act iv scene vi. And it's such a great scene, among so many great scenes. The wronged son Edgar, in disguise, is taking his blind father, Gloucester, to the cliffs at Dover where Gloucester, in despair and racked with guilt, intends to kill himself. He intends to throw himself over the edge.

But the wronged Edgar is not leading him to the cliffs of Dover. He is only pretending to. He will not assist in his father's dying. He wants his father to survive, to go on living, to feel the pain, to face the truth of what he has done, to see things feelingly, to endure. Instead of a real cliff at Dover Edgar describes an imaginary one to his father – it is a memorable reminder of what great literature can do – and one of the many unforgettable details Edgar paints (or Shakespeare paints) of the birds, the crows and choughs, and the boats and the sea below, in the midst of all that he pinpoints, as if the camera focuses in closely on him, a man riskily clinging to the cliff face, hanging there, as he picks and collects samphire: a dangerous business.

Edgar, as if giddy from the height, is here speaking to his father.

> Come on, sir. Here's the place. Stand still. How fearful
> And dizzy 'tis to cast one's eyes so low!
> The crows and choughs that wing the midway air
> Show scarce so gross as beetles. Halfway down
> Hangs one that gathers samphire—dreadful trade;
> Methinks he seems no bigger than his head:
> The fishermen that walk upon the beach,
> Appear like mice, and yond tall anchoring bark,
> Diminished to her cock, her cock a buoy
> Almost too small for sight. The murmuring surge,
> That on th'unnumbered idle pebble chafes,
> Cannot be heard so high. I'll look no more

Lest my brain turn and the deficient sight
Topple down headlong.

So, instead of ending his life in suicide from a high cliff near
Dover, Gloucester throws himself headlong forward, only to fall
flat on his face.

★

You, Clare, climb real cliffs. You look down from the summit
of real mountains, from mountain ranges, you walk on steep
coastal paths, you swim real seas around Mull up close to the
puffins, you swim to the noise from the razorbills, in turbulent
waves under dark skies, you have (as you told me) cycled much
of the length and much of the breadth of France and Spain, hot,
empty roads, and the Italian Alps, you climbed serious heights in
the Dolomites, the Via Ferrata, you trod the iron path, you have
canoed and caved, even though you hate caves, you have run
the London Marathon twice, (and you keep as a memento your
silver foil blanket), you have travelled and challenged the real
scenes of the real world.

And, in an expert way, your hands have cared for the sort of
broken.

From my desk in my hut, finding it laborious to move, but
sitting here in my swivel chair, I can swivel left to see the Edward
Thomas drawing, swivel right to see the John Betjeman statuette,
with books my adventure and books my window on the world:
I salute you.

★

I feel unsteady or light-headed when I look up, tilting my
head back as I do so, to open the curtains or to roll up the blinds
or, as today, to put the washing on the line. This is done slowly,

deliberately, clothes peg by clothes peg. Clothes peg in hand, head tilted, as if picking apples, I often come close to toppling. Well, today I toppled.

Do I tell Clare? Foolish pride holds me back. Who am I fooling?

★

Albert Speer

I have never been someone who rushes out to buy another novel about the Nazis, nor a film-goer who can't get enough of the German uniforms and the black Mercedes. Given that so many classrooms are now resounding to twentieth century war videos, and many of those centred on, if not feeding off, the Third Reich, part of me is grudgingly grateful that my own history lessons in the 1950s were mainly concerned with the Tudors and Stuarts. Even so, one book by a senior Nazi, Albert Speer's *Spandau: The Secret Diaries*, fascinated, affected and troubled me when I read it. And it haunts me still.

I first heard of it in 1976, its year of publication, the year I had finished my second novel, and I was in a spell of wondering what to write next. Indeed, being blunt, I was in a spell of asking myself did I have anything left to say (a spell I am still finding it, fifty years later, hard to shake off). Anyway, it was in this rather restless mood, reading *Encounter* magazine, soaking in my bath, that I came across a long article about Albert Speer.

I knew very little about Speer beyond the fact that he was one of the accused at the Nuremberg Trials, though I had always been fascinated by Laura Knight's vivid, desolate painting of all twenty two Nazis sitting in two rows in the dock, a group portrait of them with their headphones on. (Of the twenty-two defendants at Nuremberg, ten were condemned to death by hanging, two committed suicide, three were found not guilty, while seven – including Albert Speer – were sentenced to varying periods of time in Spandau prison.)

The article in *Encounter* took the form of an extended interview with Speer, who had been released ten years earlier after serving his twenty year sentence (1946-66) for crimes against humanity. In the years since his release from prison he had published two bestselling books: *Inside The Third Reich* (1970) and *Spandau: The Secret Diaries* (1976).

In his early career Speer was Hitler's architect (ghastly grandiose buildings) while also responsible for orchestrating the visual effects of the lurid Nuremberg rallies. For the 1937 rally, his most famous staging, Speer designed the display in which one hundred and fifty anti-aircraft searchlights (placed twelve metres apart) formed a 'Cathedral of Light' in the night sky above Zeppelin Field.

It was, however, for his conduct as Hitler's Armaments Minister from 1942, when he ruthlessly employed millions of slave labourers in the German war machine, that Speer was sentenced to his twenty years in prison. Some thought, and some still think, that he should have been hanged along with the other ten defendants. As far as the Russians were concerned, the whole twenty two of them should have been strung up.

One aspect of Speer's behaviour in prison, one feature of his psychology, captivated me from the first second I came across it in the bath. It may seem a minor detail to catch one's eye, with such large-scale horrors on view, but Speer (prisoner Number Five) took his daily exercise by going on a circular walk in the Spandau prison garden. Usually he walked alone, with only his conscience for company, and those passages in the book are of course riveting. Occasionally he was joined by one of the other prisoners for some terse exchanges (there were seven Spandau prisoners in all: Hess, Donitz, Raeder, Funk, Neurath, Schirach and Speer). Once in a while Speer might have a brief word with one of the guards he passed. The guards were Russian, French,

American and British – each nation had one month on duty, three months off – as the prison was run in an uneasy partnership by the four powers who had administered the Nuremburg trials.

A meticulous, disciplined man, Speer decided to keep an accurate record of how far he had walked during his incarceration. (You'll approve of the exercise regime, Clare, if nothing else.) So, each time Speer passed a certain point on the circuit he transferred a small bean from his left trouser pocket to his right – a strategy suggested to him by Hess – and when he returned to his cell at night he could then calculate how many kilometres he had walked by multiplying the circumference of the garden by the number of transferred beans. That sort of statistical thing appealed to Albert Speer.

But, being Speer, being dodgy, he was soon up to more than that. What would he find, he wondered, if in his mind's eye he walked straight out of the prison gates and kept on walking? If, as a free man, he could go east or west, where would his feet take him? And what would he see? He needed to find out. So, as well as doing this daily walk, come rain or shine, all the year round for twenty years, Number Five decided he would use all the resources of the prison library.

Albert Speer was an educated professional – and (an uncomfortable truth, this) there were many more of those in the Nazis than we like to think – and in his methodical way he started to take out geography and travel books on other countries, beginning with those which bordered on Germany:

> On the stretch from Saltzburg to Vienna I had to fight boredom; several times I was on the point of quitting the whole thing. Merely covering the distance no longer satisfies me. I must make it more vivid. Perhaps I should be taking the idea of hiking around the world quite literally and conceive each segment in full detail. For that purpose I would have to obtain maps and books and familiarise

myself fully with the segment that lay ahead: the landscape, the climate, the people and their culture, their occupations, their manner of life. That way I would be killing two birds with one stone. First of all I would be developing sufficient imagination in picturing what lies before me, and I should even be able to feel something like enjoyment of the novelties in store.

If he kept going, averaging his usual ten kilometres a day, Speer might even walk right round the world before his cell door was unlocked for the last time. By the day he was free to be driven away from Spandau in a black Mercedes he would know not only a lot more about the past and himself, but he would also glean a great deal about the wider world. It would be an education, and so a kind of liberation.

March 19, 1955. My fiftieth birthday.

By sheer chance, on this day I completed the last stage of the walk to Heidelberg. While I was still tramping my rounds in the garden, Hess came and sat down on his bench. It consists of two brick pedestals with a narrow board laid across them. He leaned against two tomato stakes to keep his back from touching the cold wall.

'Now I am setting out for Munich,' I said as I passed him on the next-to-last round. 'Then on to Rome and down as far as Sicily. Sicily's in the Mediterranean, so I won't be able to walk any farther.' When I had completed the last round, I stopped and sat down beside him.

'Why not by way of the Balkans to Asia?' Hess asked.

'Everything there is Communist,' I replied. 'But maybe I could go by way of Yugoslavia to Greece. And from there through Salonika, Constantinople, and Ankara to Persia.'

Hess nodded. 'That way you could reach China.'

I shook my head. 'Communist too.'

'But then across the Himalayas to Tibet.'

I turned that down too. 'Also Communist. But it would be possible to cross Afghanistan to India and Burma. The more interesting route would be through Aleppo, Beirut, Baghdad, and across the desert to Persepolis and Teheran. A long, hot tramp, lots of desert. I hope I'll find oases. At any rate, I have a good programme now. It should do me for the time being: it's a distance of four thousand kilometres. You've helped me out of an embarrassing predicament. Many, many thanks, Herr Hess.'

With a hint of a bow, as though we were at a diplomatic reception, Hess replied, 'Most pleased to be of help, Herr Speer.'

In fact Herr Speer managed 31,936 kilometres in the prison garden, a tramping feat which he drily called 'his greatest athletic achievement'. On the day of his release he finished thirty-five kilometres south of Guadalajara, in Mexico.

I found this interior/exterior walk an apt, indeed a perfect metaphor. Albert Speer was locked away in prison for his crimes against humanity but his mind was free to do as it liked, go where it liked. The walk was circular. He could choose how he examined his previous conduct and how he intended to come to a reckoning. He could either bury his head in the sand, or settle for various stages and various levels of denial (as his co-prisoners did), or he could try to face up to his conduct.

(It felt perfect material for radio drama, playing to all radio's strengths.)

Would Hitler's shadow be with him on his walk, every step of the way, would he be walking round and round with the Fuhrer with whom he had worked so closely? If so, would Speer go round and round in ever more complicit circles, spinning his self-justifying web, or would he genuinely get somewhere? Perhaps, as well as describing or explaining or explaining away what he did, he aimed to find and then to exercise his better self.

Then, there was the lavatory paper, and that merely extended the metaphor. I read that the Spandau book was based on the diaries Speer had secretly kept in his cell. The entries were written in a neat hand on sheets of lavatory paper, which he put in his shoe and then had them smuggled out of the prison. By the time he was released they ran to 25,000 pages.

The irony of Speer's daily use of lavatory paper on which to record his honest or exculpatory reflections would not have been lost on his co-defendants, not to mention the scorn the revelation would have received from Goering had he lived to find out. 'Perfect for your shit, Herr Speer! None of us ever trusted you!' Speer, after all, was the only one to plead guilty at the Nuremberg trial and he was the only one to accept, with his remorseful demeanour, the concept of collective responsibility. The others never forgave him for taking either position.

So, Number Five walks each day – to keep fit. Number Five walks each day as an imaginary release – to keep sane. Even if that was partly a survival tactic, a fit and sane and intelligent Nazi leader was rare and worth our serious attention. On each page, however, and in every chapter, I found myself asking the same question. Is Speer a decent, upper middle class family man (and father of six) who made a Faustian pact with the devil and joined Hitler's inner circle, a decision which he comes deeply to regret and for which (as a repentant sinner) he asks forgiveness, or is he a devious and cunning war criminal who would adopt or adapt or spin any subtle version he could of the 'good German' pose to save his own skin?

The question nagged.

Was I reading him correctly?

Was he doing his best to tell the truth or was he leading me and all the rest of us up the garden path, the prison garden path which he weeded so assiduously and in which he planted his own flowers and tended his own trees?

Forty-five years after I first picked it up, I have recently re-read *Spandau: The Secret Diaries* and I am yet again, as an older man, left in two (or more) minds. The book is so readable, almost seductively so. Perhaps good books do leave you in two (or more) minds. As well as the longer sequences in which Speer wrestles with his guilt, the diary grabbed me once more because it also affords intimate and arresting insights into the everyday tensions in a prison which housed some of the most notorious leaders of the Third Reich. Hess is mad (or pretending to be so, it's impossible to be sure), Admiral Donitz is unbending, Funk has his prostate problems, Schirach is shallow etc.

As well as the ongoing conflicts between the prisoners themselves, as well as the slammed doors and the clanking food bowls, there are the cellblock humiliations and regular outbursts between the prisoners and the guards, and between the prisoners and the four authorities (who also disagree amongst themselves). As a more optimistic thread, we read of Speer's relationship with Anton, the Dutch medical orderly, who never makes him feel a criminal. Indeed, the orderly offers the distressed and depressed Speer solace. There are also enlivening moments of dark humour, for example when the prisoners take offence on hearing the chaplain preach a sermon on lepers.

Though I again raced through the book I found the articulate, composed and urbane Albert Speer even more difficult to read as a man. As if he himself had come to acknowledge that inner coldness, on the very last page of his Spandau diaries Speer writes,

> Hasn't there always been a sort of wall between me and others? Has not all casualness been only a strategy to make that wall invisible?

That rings true.

People from all walks of life helped the Nazi party into power and continued to support it while increasingly appalling crimes were committed. Many of those supporters came from the solid middle classes: doctors, engineers, architects, farmers, shop-keepers, economists and, yes, plenty of schoolteachers. When I started teaching in the early 1960s, an older colleague, who had fought with distinction in the Second World War, surveyed the staff room over his coffee cup and biscuit and said quietly to me, 'We may not want to face it, Jonathan, but if this was Germany thirty years ago, some of us in this room would have been Nazis. More than a few, I'd say. Have a good look round.'

He wasn't joking. I had a good look round the room and I've been looking round ever since. With that concern partly in mind, in 1980 I wrote *The World Walk* as my first Radio 4 play and, a few years later, in a slightly different treatment, as my first television play for BBC2. The metaphor of the walk had hooked me, hooked me to radio.

★

007

-Are you ready, Mr Bond?

-Ready.

Ready I was, as ready as I could ever be, alert and alive, poised, and nicely balanced on the balls of my feet. Feet, remember. Balance. Feet, feet. Be nimble, or as nimble as you can be. Feel your toes in your shoes and in touch with the ground.

Clare was going to call out where the shots might be coming from, where the enemy marksmen were, and to know that the killers could be anywhere, at any angle or in any hiding place. And my sole aim was simple. Take them out. One by one, eliminate them. There would be no warning, no second chances.

Both my arms were now fully outstretched, braced for action, no trembling, no shaking, no tremor, holding steady my beloved Beretta .25 automatic, my gun of choice for my most dangerous missions.

-Bottom left, ground level!

-Bang!

-Behind you. Rooftop!

-Bang!

-Ninety degrees, reflection in window, left, no, right!

-Bang!

-Doorway on your left!

-Bang!

-Behind you, down!

-Bang!

-Well done.

Swivel, up, down, up, down, crouch, knees hurt, upright, down, back hurts, head swimming, heart going a hundred miles an hour, but James Bond no longer, I'm way back, back way before James Bond films, I'm back now in the tarmac suburban playground, my primary school, my father's primary school, and what's more, my mother's primary school, because she taught there too. The whole family were at the same school. No escape.

Most days, most playtimes, there were long gunfights in our yard between the boys. Cowboys and Indians. Apaches. Bang, you're dead. No, I'm not. Yes, you are. I just killed you. No, you didn't. Lie down, you're dead. Lie down or I'll smash you. You smash me and I'll smash you back. Oh, yeah? Yeah! You and whose granny?

And every year, in their season, there were the violent conker fights. You baked yours, no holds barred, you drilled a hole and fed a shoelace through and knotted it, then you baked them as hard as you could and then you smashed the other boys' conkers, smashed them to smithereens.

Girls were different.

The girls played hopscotch, with their white ankle socks hopping in and out through a number of chalked rectangles. Over near the tree some superior girls broke away from the chalked markings and skipped in a lofty self-contained style, the rope clipping the ground.

It's coming back, all of it, even the names, especially the names.

Every lunchtime Derek Ruby, the one fat boy in the school, can I still say that, the one fat boy in the school, went to the corner of the yard, stood next to the flagpole, and waved to his mother across the street. She was always there at lunchtime, waiting. She waved back, with both arms, wave, wave, and she blew him kisses. If Derek Ruby ever caught your eye watching him doing any of this he turned and changed his motherly wave into a dead-eye gun shot. He shot you dead for snooping. Bang!

Then Miss Evans, on playground duty, or Miss Jones, or my father, having been on lavatory rota, one of them blew the whistle and we all formed up in lines, quieter now, with our guns packed in our leather holsters, ready to resume our lessons.

My mother didn't let us have guns. She disapproved. No cap-guns, no Wild West clothes, no, not even water pistols. We were not allowed any gun of any description in our house. Out of sight, after school and behind her back, I played with the boys down on The Common, down where the council houses were, near the neat rows of post war prefabs, where the Wall's ice cream van parked, near where the corner shop sold gobstoppers, gobsmackers, where we roller-skated on uneven ground and swore out loud and killed each other to our hearts content, bullet after bullet. Got you! Aaarrggg!

Then home for tea and more cricket in the yard with brother David.

Mind you, my mother did not have it all her own way. Her brother, my Uncle Bert, a disabled haemophiliac, lived for some years with us. And on fine days Uncle Bert sat in the back garden in his wheelchair with his air rifle across his knees, his eye trained for rats in the chicken run. Sometimes, with a wink, and not a word spoken, he handed me the rifle and he nodded me permission, allowing me to fire a pellet or two at a disappearing rat. I always missed the target. With a steady arm and a practised eye, he rarely did.

Uncle Bert gave me my nickname, Sam. It was the only name I answered to until I went up to Cambridge, where I knew no one, and so I had to start again, and settled for my real name, Jonathan.

Uncle Bert, the one and only philosopher of my early life, moving slowly if at all, with one leg shorter than the other, was born to be called a cripple. Then the language changed. He rose slowly through the ranks of the afflicted until he was numbered among the handicapped, only to die disabled – crippled, handicapped, disabled, a career curve of a kind – and the final injustice, the final appalling irony, was that he contracted AIDS from transfusions of HIV-contaminated Factor VIII blood: one of the gravest pharmaceutical scandals of all time for which no one has ever accepted responsibility.

Uncle Bert … I have written about him before. I doubt a day passes me by without him appearing before my eyes, his cheeks Cox's orange pippin, with that straight and steady look of his, and his salutary voice in my ears. He was a hard man to live up to, Uncle Bert, and even harder to lie to. Every time I am dishonest he catches my eye.

–You did well, Clare said.

–Sorry?

–Being 007.

–Oh, that. But I bumped into the wall.

–But you didn't fall, that's the big thing. Don't run yourself down. Now, let's cross the river. Stepping up and then a big lunge over. Try it.

★

J.L.Carr

From 1949 to 1970 my father, as well as checking all was clean in the lavatories, was the head teacher of Patchway Church of England Primary School, on the A38 just north of Bristol. For many of those years, 1952-1966, the writer J.L.Carr was the head teacher of a similar school, Highfields County Primary School in Kettering, Northamptonshire. They breathed the same air, J.L.Carr and my father, the same chalky air, the chalk mingling with the smell of wooden floors and warm milk and powdery ink and smoky staff rooms and cloakrooms and pegs bulging with damp clothes. They knew all about reading ages and road safety, look right look left look right again and if all clear then cross, and they knew the daily sound of whole classes chanting their times tables. They knew the right hymns to pound out on the piano in morning assembly and the need for the loud pedal.

They both came from modest backgrounds. J.L.Carr's father was a night stationmaster. My father's father was first a cobbler, then a miner. Both my father and J.L.Carr's father went to a teacher training college, one in Dudley in the Midlands and one in Caerleon in South Wales, and both were prone to say that if you could read, write and spell the world was your oyster.

When I first read J.L.Carr's *The Harpole Report*, 1972 – which is based on his own experiences, indeed the whole novel is firmly based on his own head teacher's log – I was taken straight back to my own childhood. It is hilarious. But it is also true, true in the sense that matters, the truest book ever set in the world of a primary school. It did not reach a wide audience, however, until Frank Muir happily chose it as his book to take with him on Desert Island Discs. In more recent times, to mark the centenary of J.L.Carr's birth in 2012, I adapted the novel as a Woman's Hour Serial for BBC Radio 4. I don't think I've ever seen actors laugh more in a studio.

On every page of *The Harpole Report* I could hear my mother and my father talking. It was as if they had written it themselves: the after-school anecdotes about caretakers and stoves, concern about nit inspections and the suspect who might have been the one who left the mess on the lavatory floor, and then there were the unannounced sudden visits from Her Majesty's Inspectors, or HMIs as they were quite fearfully, no, quite respectfully, called.

George Harpole, the book's hero, is in his first term as Acting Head of Tampling St Nicholas Primary School. He has a career to make or break. He is optimistic and purposeful and his intentions are admirable, but is he up to the job? Can he handle the pupils, the parents, the staff, the governors and the local education authorities? His practical problems are wide and varied, starting first thing every morning with the dreaded caretaker, Mr Theaker.

Surrounding the Head, as of course there always will be in any primary school, are the women, a wonderful range of females. Outside the classroom but right there inside his office, Harpole has to deal with the sexually frustrated Councillor Mrs Blossom, one of the governors, pushing him up against his desk and rubbing her knees against his as she confides:

> 'Blossom is no use to me and it will be a blessing when he continues his rest elsewhere. He is absolutely no use to me in bed nor ever has been. Even in his early fifties he fell asleep the minute he hit the sack and nothing I could ever do roused him.'

Then there is the frank and infamous parent, the unhygienic Mrs Widmerpool, a rapid if reluctant breeder who explains to Harpole that she has to live with the opposite problem:

> 'Don't talk to me,' she said. 'I don't want any more. I didn't want the last three. He made me have 'em on Saturday nights. Not that now they're here

I don't think the same of them as of the first six. He won't let me be and must always be having it. Which I like and I don't like, if that makes sense to you. What I mean is I shouldn't like it if he didn't want it some time. I have seen it in my sister's love magazine that the well-off only has it of a weekend, but when I told him he said "Well, we'll go on as before and to keep up with the Joneses we'll have it twice on Sundays." '

Inside the staff room we have the 'thirty years experienced' Mrs Rita Grindle-Jones, a small town snob whose husband teaches in the local prep school and who considers the Widmerpools as not only spongers but an affront to society. 'You have not had thirty years experience, Mrs Grindle-Jones,' Harpole tells her in an outburst which prompts her early retirement, 'you have had one year's experience thirty times.'

As for the Unqualified Assistant, Miss Grace Tollemache, she is always in charge of (or 'landed with') the Backward Class. 'They know what C means even before the As and Bs and disappointed parents translate it.' In the 1950s these pupils were sometimes called ESN, the educationally subnormal, a phrase or indeed an acronym my father would not allow. In her comforting way Miss Tollemache keeps repeating 'Jesus loves us' to The Backwards:

> 'When we do good things he is happy and when we do bad things he is sad. We should not like to make him *sad*, children, should we?'
> 'No, Miss Tollemache,' they chorused.

In one of his first decisions as Acting Head, Harpole rightly abolishes the ESN class.

Most memorable of the teachers, and soon central to Harpole's day, is Miss Emma Foxberrow MA (Cantab), an untrained teacher who is as lively and free-thinking as she is emotionally unsettling to George Harpole. Her radical teaching methods fascinate and discountenance him in equal measures, while her witty asides ruffle and brighten the staff room. After school one evening, dressed in her red coat, she passes Harpole as he cycles off to the cricket nets. Balancing his large and bulky cricket bag over the handlebars, he turns to wave to her only to wobble and fall off.

Ground down by Tusker, the education officer, and frustrated at every turn by bureaucracy, yet refusing to be bullied by either Tusker or the governors, the valiant Harpole struggles on until he can take no more. He resigns over a matter of principle. This moves and inspires Miss Foxberrow, emotions which Harpole is man enough both to spot and to build his hopes on:

> 'Will you marry me, Miss Foxberrow?'
> 'No, at least not at the moment. And you may call me Emma. You may sleep with me now and then and, if we fit and all goes well, we could rationalise the arrangements for the sake of the children.'

As well as the parallels with my parents' primary school careers, there is another link: cricket. Cricket played a large part in J.L.Carr's life, as it has done in mine. He was a club cricketer until well into his sixties, a batsman who also published from home (in his Quince Tree Press), little books (five inches by three and a half inches), mostly brief selections from the English poets, perhaps no more than twenty poems or so from Marvell, Pope, Swift, Cowper, Edward Thomas, that sort of thing. But his book, *Dictionary of Extra-Ordinary Cricketers*, sold over 10,000 in a month. That was the one he wrote and illustrated himself.

Opposite page sixty-three of *The Harpole Report* (in the Quince Tree Press edition) there is an appealing black and white photograph of J.L.Carr. It tells us a lot. He is standing, in his spectacles, in his collar and tie (tie tucked into his shirt), with his jacket off and his sleeves rolled up to the elbow. He has taken his stance, with his bat, at the crease in front of three wickets chalked on the school playground wall. He looks comfortable, ready for the ball, a natural. That chap can play. He's got it. You can see it. He knows the game and he is up for it.

And looking at him in that photograph, seeing the amused expression in his eye and sensing the challenge in his half-smile, I am bowling at him, because my brother and I played cricket for hours days weeks months on end in exactly such a setting, up against three chalked stumps on our father's schoolyard wall. J.L.Carr was, I suspect, one of those Englishmen like G.F. Hardy, the great Cambridge mathematician known for his achievements in number theory, who admitted that even if he knew he was going to die today he would still want to know the county cricket scores.

In his novel *A Season in Sinji* the cricket, this time armed forces cricket, plays a large and far more dramatic part. Set on a dusty R.A.F station in West Africa during the Second World War, the action takes place in a country where J.L.Carr himself served. The story charts a personal rivalry, a rivalry to the death, between Turton, an arrogant public school officer, and Flanders, a chippy aircraftsman. The rivalry, begun in an English pub over a beautiful girl, spills over – indeed finds its expression and final resolution – in public view out on the cricket pitch in R.A.F Sinji.

There is a grown-up, uncompromising, unforgiving toughness to the novel; it is a world away in feeling from the warmth of *The Harpole Report*, with not a hero in sight. Fate is random. Here cricket (and life) is played out with a bloody-minded determination, with its deep grudges and lingering resentments, its class warfare, the North-South divide, officers versus men, amateurs v. players, indeed right down to the thorny question of who should be the captain of the team, the officer (Turton) or the better player in the ranks (Flanders).

J.L.Carr explores all this more convincingly than any novelist

I know. There are only a few works of fiction which make you believe even in village cricket, and they are mostly from the comic blacksmith genre, and only one I have read, Nathan Leamon's *The Test*, comes close to capturing the first class game.

In the cinema disbelief takes over for cricket fans the moment the first actor-bowler starts out on his Bambi run up, and disdain settles as the fielders all appeal when his inept delivery amazingly hits the stumps. Yes, they appeal. All the fielders turn to the umpire, arms aloft, and shout

How-*zat*!

No, sorry, but no. This is getting silly, so let's stop right there, shall we? Look, I know we're only one ball into the game, not even at the end of the first over, but come round, all of you, and I'll try to explain the game. Right, sit in a circle on the grass and make sure you can hear me …

Even in his description of Caroline Driffield, the girl who sparks off the whole bitter drama, J.L. Carr cannot resist a cricket analogy:

> It all boils down to this: she had style. You either have or you haven't. That's all there is to it, it's beyond doubt. Herbert Sutcliffe had it.

At the end, adrift at sea in a dinghy, dehydrating, and with the dead body of Turton beside him, Flanders bleakly reflects:

> In clearer spells, I thought how like a game of cricket this story of Turton and myself had been. Players had come and taken their stand or swung their arms and had gone. And the issue had wavered this way and that, but chiefly it had gone his way. But now the game, if you can call it that, was near its end. He had lost: that much was certain. But had I won?

So, a lifetime of classroom lessons and cricket matches ran in our blood, but in 1980 J.L.Carr produced his little masterpiece – no, not his little masterpiece, his masterpiece – and any parallels are over.

A Month in the Country is a different standard and is in a different league: not school, not village, not club, and not county. This is world class. To write as well as this you need rare understanding and rare judgement as well as a rare gift. You need an eye, a selective eye, what they call shot selection, you need timing, and of course it helps if you have that maddening ability to make it all seem so easy and so unforced, to underplay it but still to retain the heat under the simple words, to hit the ball as it goes by, to hit it just hard enough to get it to the boundary. A few cricketers have it: David Gower, that very English batsman, springs to mind.

I admire Carr's novel without reservation.

Or is it a novella?

I never know, any more than I know enough to tell how to categorise Conrad's *Heart of Darkness* or Hemingway's *The Old Man and the Sea* or Thomas Mann's *Tonio Kroger* or Paul Scott's *Staying On*. Are they long short stories or short novels or novellas? My first novel, *Wilfred and Eileen*, at just over 40,000 words, was called a novella by one critic in 1976, and for some reason that literary term made me feel a little touchy, a touch defensive. Was the critic saying that he hadn't got his money's worth, or that I couldn't develop characters or handle more than one narrative line? Perhaps he was just saying it was a novella. It's nearly fifty years ago, all that, and I should be over it by now.

Anyway, *A Month in the Country* is very short, a feature I increasingly admire in fiction. Every sentence counts. Every scene cuts at the right place. Yes, of course I still love George Eliot and Tolstoy and Dickens but perhaps because I have little time left, I find many long novels self-conscious and over-detailed and over-dressed and over-complicated and wearying even to contemplate. Just looking at them puts me off. Once finished, if they indeed ever are, many of them diminish if not drain away. On this topic, as on so many others, I find I am with Chekhov: 'Everything I read now seems not short enough.' Going back a bit, I'm also with Callimachus, the scholar and librarian in the third century BC, who said 'big book, big bore.' And while we're on about length, the late twentieth century short novel which comes closest in quality to *A Month in the Country* is Brian Moore's *Catholics*, 1972. J.L.Carr and Brian Moore, two under-rated writers.

Set in rural Yorkshire in 1920, Carr's *A Month in the Country* is centred on the village church at Oxgodby during one of those rare, hazily tranquil, undisturbed English summers, one of those spells when you think this is too good to go on and it does, one of those months when you feel lucky simply to be English.

Two war-scarred men, Tom Birkin and Charles Moon, have their private reasons to be in Oxgodby. Birkin, escaping a broken marriage, is uncovering and restoring a medieval mural in the church. While painstakingly peeling away the past, he finds himself falling in love with Alice, the lonely wife of the cold vicar, the Revd J.D.Keach. Alice comes to the church, quietly and attentively, to watch Birkin at work on the wall. Sometimes he does not hear Alice come in but he senses her presence, as you do when you are falling in love. As Berowne says in *Love's Labour's Lost*: 'A lover's ear will hear the lowest sound'. At night, and happily, Birkin sleeps on the belfry floor.

Out in his tent, close to the pit he is digging, Charles Moon has his own ghosts. Court-martialled in the war and put in the glasshouse after being found in bed with his batman – 'he was born that way' – Moon has now been commissioned by an established local family, the Hebrons, to dig for an ancient grave which may lie beyond the sanctified churchyard.

The two men scrape away. They dig, they clean, they uncover, they reflect, they touch, they reveal, they recover. Without ever noticing where we are being led by the writer, the world and how we apprehend it is somehow seen and felt in a different light. Love, longing, loss, art, memory, religion: Christian (Anglican and Methodist) and Muslim, pain, healing, sexual tension and narrative shocks … all are achieved with the lightest of brush strokes and not a wasted word. Far from diminishing, as we think about it, the book grows and grows.

In nearly every one of his novels, J.L.Carr's hero misses his moment in love, never more so than Birkin with Alice in *A Month in the Country*. And there is no second chance.

> I should have lifted an arm and taken her shoulder, turned her face and kissed her. It was that kind of day. It was why she had come. Then everything would have been different. My life, hers. We would have had to speak and say aloud what both of us knew and then, maybe, turned from the window and lain together on the makeshift bed. Afterwards we would have gone away, maybe on the next train. My heart was racing. I was breathless. She leaned on me, waiting.
>
> We can ask and ask but we can't have again what once seemed ours for ever – the way things looked, that church alone in the fields, a bed on a belfry floor, a remembered voice, the touch of a hand, a loved face. They've gone and you can only wait for the pain to pass.
>
> All this happened so long ago. And I never returned, never wrote, never met anyone who might have given me news of Oxgodby. So, in memory, it stays as I left it, a sealed room furnished by the past, airless, still, ink long dried on a put-down pen. But this was something I knew nothing of as I closed the gate and set off across the meadow.

A Month in the Country is the novel on my shelves, above all others, that I would love to have my name on. All right, *Middlemarch*, all right *Vanity Fair*, all right *The Woodlanders*, but you know what I mean: of the books I might, just might, conceivably have written.

★

'Twas a new feeling – something more
Than we had dar'd to own before,
  Which then we hid not;
We saw it in each other's eye,
And wish'd in every half-broken sigh
  To speak, but did not!

She felt my lips' impassion'd touch
'Twas the first time I dar'd so much,
  And yet, she chid not;
But whisper'd o'er my burning brow,
'Oh! do you doubt I love you now?'
  Sweet soul! I did not!

Warmly, I felt her bosom thrill,
I prest it closer, closer still,
  Though gently bid not;
Till oh! The world hath seldom heard
Of lovers, who so nearly err'd,
  And yet who – did not!

Thomas Moore (1779-1852)

A Thunderstorm in Town

She wore a new terra-cotta dress,
And we stayed, because of the pelting storm,
Within the hansom's dry recess,
Though the horse had stopped; yea, motionless
We sat on, snug and warm.

Then the downpour ceased, to my sharp sad pain
And the glass that had screened our forms before
Flew up, and out she sprang to her door;
I should have kissed her if the rain
Had lasted a minute more.

Thomas Hardy (1840-1928)

★

Dear Clare,

You got me singing. Singing my own song again. Thank you. Questions have, of course, often been asked of the nature of autobiography as a reliable source. How far can you trust any kind of autobiography or memoir or 'personal' writing, or (to go no further afield) this book? When it came to any plans for a biography of him, Henry James – a man who did not like to be jostled – said that his sole wish was 'to frustrate as utterly as possible the post-mortem exploiter.' Who wants to be a corpse to all-comers? Who wants his grave opened?

Much the same could apply to the motives of an autobiographer or memoirist. In such an impure and artful genre, how much should be taken on trust? How tempted would you be to ensure that you emerged as a decent person, to select your own anecdotes and to tell the self-fashioning story of your life (from its first humble origins) as you would like it to have been, as you *choose* it to have been (with a bit of self-censorship of intimately unwelcome disclosures and the juicier secrets), rather than as you know, deep down, it really... has been. 'Let us endeavour to see things as they are,' Dr Johnson said, 'and then enquire whether we ought to complain.'

Do you 'own' the 'facts' of your own life?

Take what happened to me in Coventry in 1998, though I hesitate to tell the story for fear of 'reading' too much into it. I had seen a documentary on TV which explored the fact that Philip Larkin was born and brought up in Coventry, so, in the spirit of *I Remember, I Remember*, I had made the trip up there to find the house where he was born. In the programme they showed a black and white photograph of his parents' place, which looked pretty gloomy, which would be about right.

Well, this wasn't to be another case of returning to a scene from the silence of the past and finding that something (in Virginia Woolf's 'magic tank') had become smaller: this was to be a case of finding nothing at all, because the whole street where Mr and Mrs Larkin and their son once lived had been demolished to make way for a ring road and an underpass. It was distressing and funny and apt.

With time on my hands, and not wanting to waste the whole day – and I cannot explain why I did this because I have no interest in cars – I bought a ticket and wandered into The Museum of British Road Transport. I drifted from room to room, feeling pointless, barely focusing, ambling through the display, through the 1910s and 1920s and 1930s, there were cars from every decade of the twentieth century, past an Alvis, past a Riley, past shiny grilles and polished radiators and on my way to Thrust 2, when it happened.

At first I thought it was just an uncanny trick of the light or, worse, the photophobic beginnings of another migraine that could well further spoil my day. Then the recognition, the familiarity and the disorientation hit me immediately. I looked around, half spun around rather, nearly losing my balance as I saw them – one, then another, and unbelievably another – form a group around me, a threatening group even, as if someone was playing a nasty trick on me by copying and reproducing the stages, if not the very shape, of my life.

I steadied myself and looked again.

They were same models, and even more disturbing, they were all the right colours. One, two, three… Seven of them in fact. The Mini Minor was the first to catch my eye, the first explosion, my first car, and it was the same powder blue as mine, registration number AHT 371 B, the car I drove off to Edinburgh in for my first job. But what about the back seat? That was where my eye went, to the back seat, which I was always thinking about for the last hour I was in the pub: no room at all, hopeless for girls.

Then the rest went off like a cluster bomb. Just to the left of my Mini there was a 1933 Hillman, exactly the same as Dad's, black and red, the first car Dad ever bought, and I was nine in the back seat and on the way to our holidays in North Wales. I could hear the way the wipers squeaked and dragged when it was raining.

My heart was starting to bump. My eyes, trying to escape, flicked the other way only to see all the other cars I had ever owned, all grouped together.

I stumbled on round the museum. Anywhere. It didn't matter where, I just walked, seeing nothing clearly now, just cars, other cars, other people's cars, any old cars, other pieces of rubber and metal, that's what they were after all, not personal phantoms but pointless pieces of metal, that's all they were, the make and the model and the colour didn't matter, they were lumps of rubber and metal rescued from the scrapyard, boring bloody cars.

Exhibition pieces.

Museum pieces.

They meant nothing to me.

I left the museum straight away. I did not go back and look closely again at any of the cars to check dispassionately what I had seen. I did not walk round them or peer in the windows or remind myself of their distinguishing features. There was no need. I was inside them. I could smell each of them. I could feel them. I could touch and smell and see and feel the people in them and the lives they led, the lives we led, the histories, the comedies, (the tragedies too), the rooms, the walls, the bedside tables, the minds and the bodies.

In setting out to find a bit of Philip Larkin's past I had stumbled upon my own. I am trying to tell it as it was and is, but if I take the photos off the wall, if I reach up with both my hands and carefully unhook the old framed photographs, will the swirling pattern of wallpaper behind each of them still be as new, still as fresh, and still as unfaded as on the day of my birth in war time Gloucester?

★

I remember, I remember
The house where I was born,
The little window where the sun
Came peeping in at morn;
He never came a wink too soon
Nor brought too long a day;
But now, I often wish the night
Had borne my breath away.

I remember, I remember
The roses red and white,
The violets and the lily cups--
Those flowers made of light!
The lilacs where the robin built,
And where my brother set
The laburnum on his birthday,
The tree is living yet!

I remember, I remember
Where I was used to swing,
And thought the air must rush as fresh
To swallows on the wing;
My spirit flew in feathers then
That is so heavy now,
The summer pools could hardly cool
The fever on my brow.

I remember, I remember
The fir-trees dark and high;
I used to think their slender tops
Were close against the sky:
It was a childish ignorance,
But now 'tis little joy
To know I'm farther off from Heaven
Than when I was a boy.

Thomas Hood (1799-1845)

★

Today I had an appointment – a check-up, a where-are-we-at, not exactly a progress report – with a consultant. (I nearly wrote *my* consultant but that would be to give the wrong impression.) Anyway, I liked the woman doctor I met for the first time today. For a start she looked straight at me rather than at the computer screen. She was warm and quick and she was fun. And every now and then, while checking my balance, do I need a stick, she tried to unbalance me, to push me over, checking my too high blood pressure and my medication and asking me about my latest symptoms and giddiness and exercise regimes, before she gave me another big nudge with her elbow, leaning on me as if we were in on a private joke. Perhaps we were. Things could be worse. I can still walk. I've still got two legs.

Another nudge from my consultant.

Don't tell me she fancies me?

Don't be silly.

I found myself being funny, flirting, I could feel myself performing, coming alive. I could feel my blood buzzing.

★

Long John Silver

In 1873 a one-legged poet from Gloucester set off, leaning on his crutch, for far away Edinburgh. His purpose: to establish himself as a patient of Professor Joseph Lister at the Edinburgh Infirmary, and so to increase his chances of saving his 'good' leg. Professor Lister (1827-1912) was the father of modern antisepsis. He had pioneered sterile surgery: wash your hands, he insisted, wear clean gloves, spray and sterilise the instruments, and reduce the incidence of infection and gangrene.

W.E. Henley had lost one leg as a young boy – more disability, I'm afraid, but more creativity too – and Henley was now, at twenty-four, in danger of losing his other tubercular arthritic foot. Professor Lister was his last and best chance.

> I have passed through deep waters since last I picked up my pen. Here's the inventory. Wednesday 20th August I set off from Wapping. Thursday 21st, going north, I am somewhat sea-sick. Friday 22nd August, cold and wet, I land at Leith, cab it hither to the Infirmary, am informed by Mr Lister that probably my foot'll have to come off, and am put to bed in the reserved ward.
>
> It is a small dark room, a kind of back kitchen. There is a bed. There are two chairs, a worn out rickety table and stool, an illumination, and a sheaf of hymns hung on a plaster. It's a Calvinist's cell, all right, with no books, no grog and no company.

I can see myself getting only into interminable monologues. I shall become a very Hamlet.

Henley, the hard-drinking son of a bookseller, was an extrovert; he was a bellowing fellow, flamboyant and brave. With his red hair and tangled beard and strongly expressed views he made an impression wherever he went, and that was his intention. He had presence. (There are some character parallels here with the painter Alfred Munnings, about whom I have already written.)

Henley spent fifteen months at the Infirmary under Professor Lister, enduring harrowing medical procedures which he described in his collection *Hospital Sketches*. In these direct poems we see everything from Henley's bed, from a life of pain lived on one's back. While not as shocking as Fanny Burney's account of her mastectomy sixty years earlier – when you want to look away but can't – these stoical poems of Henley's are some of the finest written from a patient's point of view. Set in a back room at the Edinburgh Infirmary in 1873, with Henley's foot 'a brilliant, hideous red,' swaddled in wet white lint, even Dickens does not seem melodramatic. Would Henley end up as a trunk and no more?

> Hist? ...
> Through the corridor's echoes,
> Louder and nearer
> Comes a great shuffling of feet.
> Quick, every one of you,
> Straighten your quilts, and be decent!
> Here's the Professor ...
>
> You are carried in a basket,
> Like a carcass from the shambles,
> To the theatre, a cockpit
> Where they stretch you on a table.

Then they bid you close your eyelids,
And they mask you with a napkin,
And the anaesthetic reaches
Hot and subtle through your being.

And you gasp and reel and shudder
In a rushing, swaying rapture,
While the voices at your elbow
Fade – receding – fainter – farther.

Lights about you shower and tumble,
And your blood seems crystallising –
Edged and vibrant, yet within you
Racked and hurried back and forward.

Then the lights grow fast and furious,
And you hear a noise of waters,
And you wrestle, blind and dizzy,
In an agony of effort,

Till a sudden lull accepts you,
And you sound an utter darkness …
And awaken … with a struggle …
On a hushed, attentive audience.

He awakes to see Professor Lister leaning over him:

His face at once benign and proud and shy,
If envy scout, if ignorance deny,
His faultless patience, his unyielding skill,
Innumerable gratitudes reply.
His wise, rare smile is sweet with certainties,
And seems in all his patients to compel
Such love and faith as failure cannot quell.

Lister had exposed the affected bone, made a long cut dividing
the vessels, tendons, everything, made a triangular cavity and

scooped out the damage. Then he had filled the cavity with two inch strips of lint steeped in carbolic acid.

As well as the Professor, there was another regular visitor at Henley's bedside, a man who would soon become even more famous than the surgeon. Robert Louis Stevenson, a raffish bohemian one year younger than Henley, had heard that the poet from Gloucester was in the Infirmary and he called, along with Leslie Stephen (the editor of Cornhill Magazine), to see him. They hit it off and quickly became firm, warm and uninhibited friends.

Henley and Stevenson were amused by each other's deliberately provocative remarks. Riotous, scornful and intrepid, they liked Balzac and Baudelaire and Hugo and Dumas. Irresponsible and unmarried, they mocked orderliness and respectability and hated sham goodness and those who mouthed moralities. They both liked a rattling good read. Swift and edgy, fast and blast – that was their spoken and written style. Restless as a spaniel, Stevenson paced around the back room laughing as Henley bubbled his bile into the blue air.

They made a rare fine sight in the hospital. Stevenson:

> valiant in velvet, with his look-at-me straw hat, neat-footed and weak-fingered, bold-lipped, slight unspeakably, more a lass than a lad, a lover and sensualist, walking as lightly as Ariel, with a streak of Puck, Hamlet most of all.

Henley, a roaring buccaneer with a face like a ham and listing like a ship, read his poems aloud to Stevenson who thought them 'damned fine.' They all 'rang true.' They 'moved him to the soles of his shoes.'

The two had another deep bond, possibly even deeper than their taste in books. Both men suffered from chronic health problems. As well as his other issues, Henley had a disabled hand, and he confided in Stevenson that he had a huge ulcer on his stump as big as a sovereign and a testicle swollen to over twice its size. Stevenson, for his part, had tuberculosis and suffered frequent haemorrhages. (I sometimes wonder what physiotherapy you would have set in train, Clare, for the two of them.)

A mutual dependency developed, positive and spirited, and in the course of the next few years Henley's encouragement of Stevenson, giving him the 'little push' that all writers need, helped the young Scot to make his mark. Henley drew attention to Stevenson's work in the *Magazine of Art*, *The New Review* and *The Scots Observer*, all of which (at various times) he edited with courage and panache.

Released from the Edinburgh Infirmary, maimed but serviceable, Henley left Lister and the old grey city and its stony streets for the London literary and art world. Rigged up on a couch he worked himself very hard, an indefatigable and defiant force with his blue pencil. He was a wounded Achilles, a Philoctetes. *Clarify and strain*, he told his writers, a marvellous piece of advice, *clarify and strain*. He introduced Stevenson to Chatto and Windus and championed the sculptor Auguste Rodin years before the French academic art establishment would come to accept him. As testament to this, Rodin's bronze busts of W.E. Henley, to whom Rodin owed so much, can be seen in the National Portrait Gallery and in the crypt of St Paul's Cathedral.

★

Many of us, I imagine, know the feeling of a friendship slipping away, of sensing a good friend has 'moved on' and won't be calling any more, and the lying awake at all hours wondering whether the cause or the blame, if blame there is, rests with us. Whenever I think of Henley and Stevenson I recall Brutus's lines in Act IV scene 2 of *Julius Caesar* on hearing from Lucilius how much Cassius's manner has changed:

> Thou hast described
> A hot friend cooling. Ever note, Lucilius,
> When love begins to sicken and decay
> It useth an enforced ceremony.

Three factors caused the cooling, then the final breach, between the bosom friends Henley and Stevenson: Stevenson's marriage in 1880 in San Francisco; the publication of his most famous novel in 1883; and in 1888 a clear accusation of plagiarism.

In 1880, shortly after her divorce, Stevenson married Fanny Van de Grift Osbourne, an American ten years his senior. They were deeply in love and remained so throughout their marriage. Fanny was a strong woman and increasingly protective of her husband, particularly as his health steadily deteriorated. R.L.S thought Fanny's eyes as of 'gold and brambledew'; W.E.H thought her 'a little watchdog with the eyes of a man sighting a pistol.'

For her part, Fanny considered the heavy-drinking and over-powering Henley a bad influence on her Louis (she called him *Loo-eee*, Henley stuck to *Lew-is*). The two writers had already collaborated, at Henley's insistence, on four unsuccessful plays. On top of that, Henley was borrowing money from them. The last thing, in Fanny's view, that her gaunt Louis needed – with his sciatica, his ophthalmia and his morphine for his consumptive blood-spattered coughing – was any further dissipation with his foul-mouthed friend.

Marriage, as it sometimes does, puts old friends to the door.

Secondly, in 1883, Stevenson published *Treasure Island*, which he had written in one inspired month. It is a great, exhilarating novel – my father read it to me, I have recently read it aloud to my grandson – and it has never been out of print, a thrilling romance that brought the 'jingling, tingling, golden-minted quid' rolling in. Stevenson described its inception:

> I made the map of an island. It was elaborately and (I thought) beautifully coloured: the shape of it took my fancy beyond expression; it contained harbours that pleased me like sonnets and with the consciousness of the predestined I ticketed my performance *Treasure Island*. As I pored over my map the future characters of the story began to appear there visibly among imaginary woods – Jim Hawkins, Captain Smollett and Long John Silver.
>
> I had some paper before me and soon was writing out a list of chapters. How often have I done so before and the thing gone no further, but there seemed an element of success about this enterprise. It was to be a story for boys, no need for psychology or fine writing.

And from the novel:

> As for Long John Silver, how that personage haunted my dreams, I need scarcely tell you. On stormy nights, when the wind shook the four corners of the house, and the surf roared along the cove and up the cliffs, I would see him in a thousand forms and with a thousand diabolical expressions.
>
> His left leg was cut off close by the hip, and under his left shoulder he carried a crutch, which he managed with wonderful dexterity, hopping upon it like a bird. He was very tall and strong, with a face as a big as a ham, plain and pale but intelligent and smiling.

It was not, you might say, difficult for Henley, however drunk he was, to spot something here. Yo-ho-ho and a bottle of rum.

The *roman à clef* or *livre à clef* has a track record in the English novel, as by the sound of the phrases it must do in French, and no doubt other languages. Feeding too closely off friends and acquaintances is, of course, an occupational temptation and an occupational hazard for novelists. Thomas Love Peacock mocked and caricatured Coleridge (Mr Flosky), Byron (Mr Cypress) and Shelley (Mr Glowry) in his Gothic satire *Nightmare Abbey*, while Disraeli and Somerset Maugham often lifted their characters from prominent figures of their day, barely bothering to disguise them. In any company, however, Stevenson's appropriating portrait of Long John Silver stands out.

Nor did Henley welcome with open arms Stevenson's *faux naïf* admission and confession that it was 'the sight of your maimed strength and masterfulness that begot John Silver in *Treasure Island*. Of course he is not in any other quality or feature the least like you.' (Oh no, not in the least.) 'But you were always larger than life and bolder than bold.'

With a merry word and a slap on the shoulder, Henley had been turned into a 'character.' Deeply wounded, he probably jumped to the wrong conclusion: that the meddlesome minx Fanny was to blame, the wife who had coddled and changed her '*Loo-eee*' and turned him against his old friend. Henley felt he was no longer needed.

> The spring, my dear,
> Is no longer spring.
> Does the blackbird sing
> What he sang last year?
> Are the skies the old
> Immemorial blue?
> Or am I, or are you,
> Grown cold?
>
> O Time and Change, they range and range
> From sunshine round to thunder!

They glance and go as the great winds blow,
And the best of our dreams drive under.
For Time and Change estrange, estrange –
And now they have looked and seen us,
O, we that were dear, we are all-too near
With the thick of the world between us.

Thirdly, Fanny Osbourne Stevenson was something of a writer herself, a misguided view in which she was sometimes encouraged by her loving husband, as loving husbands sometimes will. She wrote short stories. When Henley read one of them he was shocked. He knew it. He picked up his pen and pointed out in a letter to Stevenson that *The Nixie*, one of Fanny's short stories printed in Scribner's Magazine in New York in March 1888, was far too close to one written by Stevenson's cousin Katharine de Mattos, a story that Katharine had read out to them the last time they had all met:

> It is Katharine's. Surely it is Katharine's? The situation, the environment, the principal figure – *voyons!* There are even reminiscences of phrases and imagery, parallel incidents –

The expected letter came back from Saranac Lake, New York State:

> My dear Henley,
> I write with indescribable difficulty, and if not with perfect temper you are to remember how very rarely a husband is expected to receive such accusations against his wife...
> From the bottom of my soul I believe what you wrote to have been merely reckless words written in forgetfulness, and with no clear appreciation of their meaning, but it is hard to think that anyone – and least of all my friend – should be so careless ...

To have inflicted more distress than you have done would have been difficult. This is the sixth or seventh attempt I make to write to you, and I will now only count upon you immediately applying to Katharine for the facts, and await your answer with the most painful expectation. You will pardon me if I can find no form of signature. I pray God such a blank will not be of long endurance.

Robert Louis Stevenson.

It was all over.

The final exchanges in this sad business can be found in the form of a poem by Henley and a fable by Stevenson:

> Friends ... old friends ...
> One sees how it ends.
> A woman looks
> Or a man lies,
> And the pleasant brooks
> And the quiet skies,
> Ruined with brawling
> And caterwauling,
> Enchant no more
> As they did before.
> And so it ends
> With friends.
>
> Friends ... old friends...
> And what if it ends?
> Shall we dare to shirk
> What we live to learn?
> It has done its work,
> It has served its turn;
> And, forgive and forget
> Or hanker and fret,
> We can be no more
> As we were before.

When it ends, it ends
With friends.

Friends… old friends…
So it breaks, so it ends.
There let it rest!
It has fought and won,
And is still the best
That either has done.
Each as he stands
The work of its hands,
Which shall be more
As he was before?
What is it ends
With friends?

A fable

A man quarrelled with his friend.

'I have been much deceived in you,' said the man.

And the friend made a face and went away. A little after, they both died, and came together before the great white Justice of the Peace. It began to look black for the friend, but the man for a while had a clear character and was getting in good spirits.

'I find here some records of a quarrel?' said the Justice, looking at his notes. 'Which of you was in the wrong?'

'He was,' spoke the man. 'He spoke ill of me behind my back.'

'Did he so?" said the Justice. 'And how, pray, did he speak of your neighbours?'

'Oh, he always had a nasty tongue,' said the man.

'And you chose him for your friend?' cried the Justice. 'My friend, we have no use here for fools.'

So the man was cast into the pit, and the friend laughed aloud in the dark and remained to be tried on other charges.

★

I was lying face down on the plinth, with Clare's hands, strong and skilful, at work on my shoulders and back. She unlocks and restores. She has the touch, a touch that also leads to a deeper openness. In that spirit, we had been talking for a while about why I have been prone to shy away from facing disability, then about my self-consciousness, and after that spell of vulnerable openness we both settled, as one often does, for a little silence.

Besides, I was now in the habit, almost the routine, of sending her my new chapters. She was my new reader, the reader I was most writing for. She had loosened me up without knowing what I was secretly about.

Would she be interested in the novels of Anthony Powell, I wondered, or had the world moved on, leaving him on the Acquired Taste bookshelf? Well, it felt a long shot: Powell was certainly not everyone's cup of tea.

–Any easier? The right shoulder?

–Yes, very much so. But please keep going.

–There?

–Ouch. That's the spot.

–There?

–Right there.

Also, my back had been troublesome, the same old story, and backs can be a real bugger as we all know, and I was all geared up for a bit of my bloody back moaning, but to cut that short I only had to think for a moment of W.E.Henley lying in the Edinburgh Infirmary for a year, or, for a lifetime, bedbound Uncle Bert.

★

Defying micrographia, and hoping Uncle Bert would be proud of me for doing so, today I covered a whole page with my signature.

★

Llwyncyntefin

We all dread 'losing' someone: a parent, a partner, a lover, a friend, perhaps most of all a child. It has been an almost daily fear of mine, a resident anxiety. It is a fact of life that I suspect many of us find difficult to accept, that many of us struggle to reach a philosophical accommodation with death. Somehow, like Philip Larkin, we can always hear the ambulance siren in the distance, but coming our way, reminding us that all streets in time are visited, reminding us that every day brings something a little closer that has to come. Of course I know there's no escape. I'm not that stupid. I also know that I have an incurable disease. There's no need to tell me, I know we all have a rendezvous with *Death/At some disputed barricade*, but the very thought of extinction and what my imagination does with it, strikes me as almost unbearable.

When it came to losing my parents, their ashes were scattered in Wales, in the River Usk at Sennybridge, a village in Powys. In 1995 my mother scattered the remains of my father, and when my mother died in 2001 my brother David and I scattered hers under Llwyncyntefin Bridge, a few hundred yards downstream from where the Senni flows into the Usk. We took it in turns to shake the urn empty.

For many years that old stone bridge was a special place for my family. Though much smaller in scale, it is the sort of spot that Wordsworth (had he been Welsh) would surely have set one of his great poems. After heavy rains it can be a kind of tumultuous brook of Greenhead Ghyll, though never on the scale of the Wye at Tintern Abbey or a Kirkstone Pass. We walked in all weathers and all seasons along the banks of the Senni and of the Usk, ducking under low branches, scouring for the kind of stones that might lightly skim their way to the other side. On dry days the river ran translucent; in rainy spells the river bulged and muddied itself.

Leaving the cricket bat and the yellow tennis ball in the grass on the bank, we sat quietly on an outcrop, passing the binoculars around, waiting for something to make our day, watching the dippers bobbing and jerking their tails up and down before they walked right into the water and then under the water and along the bed of the stream. Does any other bird behave quite like that?

Despite the bridge's enduring appeal, I sometimes wish with an unexpected pang that my parents were buried side by side in Rhydybriw Churchyard overlooking the Usk. That was the church where my father (dark-suited) read the lesson every Sunday morning. My mother never went, preferring to stay stolidly in her armchair by the hearth. Of the family, only my daughter Becky joined my father in church. It would be good, though, to stand somewhere, not to mope but in the knowledge that Dad and Mum were underfoot, right there, to stand and remember and thank them. I have no religion, and the unceasing cleansing river, always different, always the same, is the right and proper metaphor for my sense of time and memory, but to be honest I still miss having them in a specifically earthy place. Yet again I find myself in a logical muddle: in a similar way, although not a Christian myself, I always liked teaching in a Christian school.

Llwyncyntefin Bridge is just off the A40 in Sennybridge. You take the B road to Petrefelin and Pentre Bach. The bridge has a high arch and broad walls and bends a little in the middle, and it is very narrow, just wide enough for a hill farmer in his Land Rover and trailer to bring some cattle down to the market, and just narrow enough, if you've had a couple too many at the Shoemakers Arms in Pentre Bach, to scrape the side of your car.

It wasn't just dippers down at the water's edge. There were the running grey wagtails, scurrying and snapping up the gnats, some speedy swallows swooping low, a patient heron often stock still on a boulder where the river opened out, and once in a while a darting kingfisher would flash past.

And to complicate things, to offset any chance of this country scene becoming too cosy a romantic seclusion, it was irregularly disturbed by a noisy helicopter barging and banging its way in to land, heavy, hovering, kicking up dust and slowly settling its bulky weight on the landing pad. Or a pair of low-flying jets would scream and roar over the foothills of the Brecon Beacons, did you see them, no, your eyes and ears are out of sync, too slow, you looked at the wrong part of the sky and they had gone before you could get a proper sighting.

Because, our spot had the Sennybridge Army Camp as a serious backdrop. It is a large Ministry of Defence area full, over the years, of troops on their way to tours of duty in Northern Ireland or the Falklands or Iraq or to be deployed to Afghanistan. Or wherever they were sent. We passed the soldiers every day, some still boys, with all the kit, the packs, the sweat, the tanned arms, the tattoos, the route marches, the rifles, the camouflage and the walkie-talkies. In the busy Camp Shop, over frothy coffee and doughnuts, you heard every accent in the British Isles.

★

Some of the soldiers did seem to me more boys than men – what I think of as sixth form boys rather than squaddies or riflemen – and for some, a maudlin thought, Sennybridge could well have been their final training. I am thinking of young soldiers like Arthur, Hads and Taff, the three Bristol boys in Owen Sheers's gut-wrenching verse drama *Pink Mist* (2013). Owen Sheers, by the way, comes from Abergavenny, a town also on the Usk and only twenty odd miles east along the A40.

Once you've met Arthur, Hads and Taff you will not forget

them. At primary school, as three little boys, a little gang, they liked to link arms. As teenagers and a bit further down the track, they had to get out of the Bristol they knew, they had get away from the high rise flats and the crap apprentice pay, and one day they thought why not be three recruits, yes, why not, they had the combat itch and they wanted to stick together and to stir things up.

So they enlisted together as mates and went off to Catterick. And Afghanistan. While the boys make their hasty decision to exchange their sports bags for battledress and Catterick for Afghanistan, their loved ones – a girlfriend, a mother and a wife – act as a chorus.

Arthur, Hads and Taff don't *come home proper* from Afghanistan. In truth the three mates are taken apart, and the truth is messy. Arthur is killed. Taff, injured but not too seriously, is back in England, where he hits the bottle and the pills, attacks someone in a pub with a glass and does a year for GBH. Inside prison, Taff even misses Arthur's funeral. As for Hads he is a double amputee. He's left on two stumps, which is one stump more than W.E.Henley, stumps with raised pink scars, now half a tall man, heading back to the Headley Court Rehabilitation Centre. The burns on his back will heal in time but something else has been hurt, something which the surgeons can't reach. Even so, half gone half left, Hads is soldiering on, partly for himself, partly for his Mum, resolving *to make the living I'd got left worthwhile.*

And the title?

Pink Mist is a direct hit.

I also saw the stage version in 2017.

Pink Mist is when one of your friends goes in a flash or a fireball. Now you see your mate, now you don't. Now he's next to you, now he's just scattered bits and pieces, identified by part of an arm with a coiling dragon tattoo.

★

Our sleep in Sennybridge was sometimes disturbed by pounding feet coming up the lane. You could hear them running, loud boots, army-style, crunching past our place in the pitch black and fading away up to the artillery range on the Mynydd Epynt, a mountain moorland plateau to the north. Did they, I used to wonder, need those night vision goggles up there?

Twelve thousand hectares of the Epynt were acquisitioned by the military in 1940, soon after the outbreak of the Second World War, uprooting and displacing a close-knit hill-farming community of fifty-four homes and two hundred and nineteen people, closing the church, the primary school and the Drovers Arms.

If the wind was in the right quarter, on a walk you could sometimes just catch the booms of the big guns and the mortars. Up there the soldiers, perhaps Hads and Arthur and Taff, would be trained to storm or raid or infiltrate the mocked-up town. In the middle of that wild open country, streets and houses had been specially built by the army to familiarise the troops with the kind of operational territory they could expect 'on the ground' in house-to-house Belfast or when checking out part of a bombed block in Helmand Province. This was practice for when they encountered an enemy unit or a nest of the Taliban. The real deal.

Who knew what was coming the soldiers' way? It might be a roadside bomb, tracer fire and rockets, a sniper's bullet, a flash in the bushes or an IED, an improvised explosive device. I did manage to get up close to the mocked-up town in the training area once, on a minor trespass with my father who knew his way along the old drovers' roads on the Epynt. The place was a bit like an old Hollywood film set.

By the way, it was when we were climbing a mountain in the Brecon Beacons – Cribyn, in fact – that I told the children I had a photograph somewhere of me saluting Field Marshal

Bernard Montgomery of Alamein, KG, GCB, DSO, PB. They just laughed, yeah, yeah, yeah, Dad, and then there's the one of you and Rommel in a tank in the desert, and of course I couldn't find the Monty evidence anywhere. It turned up last winter, though, when we were going through piles of papers and photographs in the cellar, so for the proof that I was telling the truth, that their father wasn't a fantasist, they had to wait forty odd years.

Anyway, Llwyncyntefin Bridge, the bridge over the Usk, was the place where the children spent many of their afternoon hours in the 1980s. They jumped from dry rock to dry rock or from slippery moss-covered rock to slippery moss-covered rock, trying to get right under the bridge and out the other side without falling into the cold water. As many children do, they named the outcrops after the continents or even a few individual islands: Africa and Madagascar, Australia and New Zealand, and always India. Ask them now, years later, and they are still competitively specific on how dependent the visible geography was on the precise level of the river, the recent rains, the colour of the water and the time of year. It was a world as familiar to them as their bedrooms.

Out walking in Wales, they liked to wear their grandfather's old clothes. Apart from on Sundays, all his clothes were brown and green: his old check waistcoats, his old check flat caps, and you had to have a stick with you, one he had cut from one of the hedgerows on the lanes and individually labelled in his green tape. You needed a stick to clear a way through the cow parsley or to beat down the tall nettles (wet and dusty *to prove the sweetness of a shower*), nettles which spread aggressively and grew larger and more dominant by the day. Turn your back for a week in mid-summer and the nettles could close off a path.

And, of course, it was over those rocks and continents and under that bridge that their grandparents' ashes later floated. And the river, as Tennyson suggests, goes on for ever:

I chatter over stony ways,
    In little sharps and trebles,
I bubble into eddying bays,
    I babble on the pebbles.

With many a curve my banks I fret
    By many a field and fallow,
And many a fairy foreland set
    With willow-weed and mallow.

I chatter, chatter, as I flow
    To join the brimming river,
For men may come and men may go
    But I go on for ever.

A few months ago my daughter sent me a photo of her and my grand-daughter, now twenty-one, standing together on the same Welsh bridge.

★

I am finding swallowing difficult.

★

Lord Moran and the Hippocratic oath

'The truth is messy,' V.S. Naipaul said. 'It is not pretty. Writing must reflect that. Art must tell the truth.'

Those words, about as true as you can be about the truth, bring to mind Lord Moran's controversial book, *Churchill: the Struggle for Survival* (1966). From 1940 – from the critical moment when Churchill, aged sixty-five, became the wartime Prime Minister – until his death in 1965, Lord Moran was Churchill's doctor and a regular attendant on his travels at home and abroad.

For Churchill's last twenty-five years (both in and out of Downing Street) Lord Moran saw his famous patient – or *the old carcass*, as Churchill liked to describe himself – through everything that advancing age and decrepitude could throw at him: strokes, bouts of pneumonia, heart scares, diverticulitis, a rupture, depressions and mood swings, not to mention palpitations, conjunctivitis, throat problems, heavy colds, wobbly knees and tingly fingers. Sometimes under pressure from his patient, the doctor prescribed phergan, bellergal, aminophyline, disprins, immenoctal and seconal, not to mention a whole range of red and white pills, capsules and sachets. The red pep pills Churchill called his 'Morans.' But, in all this, we must be careful, as Peter Hennessy warned, not to turn 'the old warrior into a kind of walking off-licence-cum-pharmacy.'

Throughout those twenty five years Lord Moran kept a diary, though this was strictly forbidden, and the exact nature of 'the diary' is much debated. Barely one year (hardly a decent interval) after Churchill had been buried in Bladon churchyard, the doctor published his long, detailed and intimate account – it ran to over eight hundred pages – of those decades of caring for and observing at the closest quarters the indispensable man.

Churchill: the Struggle for Survival was far more than a carefully documented medical history by a man who thought he was an insider. With its revealing bedside anecdotes and its insights into history and politics and events on the great stage it was a sensation.

On its publication there was an indignant uproar, not only from the medical profession, and not only in the letters pages of *The Times*. Randolph Churchill and Mary Soames, Churchill's only son and his youngest daughter, were outraged and incensed, seeing the whole project as an inexcusable breach of a doctor's ethics, in particular by one who had been considered by the family not only a distinguished physician but an old and trusted friend. The Churchills never forgave Moran. The book was a betrayal of confidence. Quite apart from anything else, the frailties and indignities of old age had, in great detail, been indecently shown.

Other famous figures, who had played their part at various times on the public stage, also did not like the quotes or the attitudes attributed to them. They distanced themselves from the book, challenging not only the ethical position of the doctor-turned-diarist but the accuracy of Moran's accounts.

Critics on all sides reached for their translations of the Hippocratic Oath:

> *Whatsoever things I see or hear concerning the lives of men in my attendance on the sick or even apart therefrom which ought not to be noised abroad I will keep silence thereon counting such things to be as sacred secrets.*
> (from the original version)

> *I will respect the privacy of my patients, for their problems are not disclosed to me that the world may know. Most especially must I tread with care in matters of life and death.*
> (from the modern version)

Whatever the rights and wrongs of this frank and intimate publication – and there is conflicting evidence over whether it was soundly based on a daily diary or on notes or on retrospective reflections or was a fusion but essentially truthful mixture of all these – there is no doubt that Moran can write. As a boy his ambition had always been to write and write he can. It is (to my taste) by any standards a very long book but I could not stop turning the pages.

To take a step back: who was Lord Moran and how did he arrive at his privileged position?

Born in 1882 – he was eight years younger than Churchill – Charles Wilson (later Lord Moran) came from modest Northern

Irish stock. The son of a doctor, and with no important social connections, he was brought up in Skipton, Yorkshire, and educated at Pocklington School. It was an ascetic, conventional upbringing and its puritanical influence stayed with him. After one dry sherry he would put his hand firmly over his glass. He made it plain he preferred cold water. It was important always to have a clear head. As Churchill was squirting a bit more soda into his own brandy, he liked to tease Moran, saying he would have made a good monk.

Charles Wilson may have hoped one day to be a writer but he claimed life for him really began when he went to St Mary's Hospital, London. And it was to St Mary's that he dedicated his relentless energy and his formidable drive – as a doctor, as a fearless rugby player, as team captain on and off the pitch, before becoming a dominating and long-serving Dean there. He was an enemy of the incompetent. He did not mind rocking boats. He could be cantankerous. You did not easily deflect him. More than anyone, as an administrator, leader and fundraiser, he rebuilt the St Mary's medical school and he reshaped the hospital's destiny.

Moran had a nose, a sharp nose, for medical power and for medical politics. He liked to win on hospital committees as much as on the field of play. (He called a tedious committee he was on as 'a group of flats with one sharp': himself of course). He liked to win on his own merits. He liked sitting on top table. If he had gone into the church or into education he would have been a bishop or a headmaster. He was knighted in 1938. In 1941 he was elected the President of the Royal College of Physicians and then created Baron Moran in 1943. He was an ambitious young man and he was an ambitious old man.

Charles Wilson's time as a young officer in the trenches (1914–1917) gave him, after many years reflection, his first book, *The Anatomy of Courage* (1945). He was regimental medical officer to the 1st Battalion the Royal Fusiliers, and for over a thousand days of continuous danger, and repeatedly under bombardment, he was responsible for a thousand men. Each morning at medical parade it was Moran's job to decide whether to send someone down the line with shell shock or to send them back to the front for more action. Effectively he was deciding whether many men would live or die. It was a responsibility he felt deeply for the rest of his life.

In the trenches Moran came to understand the birth of fear. He came to understand that the soldier is alone with his terror, and to see that courage is victory over fear not an absence of fear: each person has a finite amount of courage. Your courage, Moran observed, could be spent. Some stick at it longer than others, some do keep going, but sooner or later all break. It was not just a matter of physical strength or rugby-style bravery. You could be 'a sticker' but your mind could be hurt beyond endurance. There is, he found, no crude scale for measuring these things or for assessing the men who endured it. It is not the case that the world divides up into those who are brave and those who are windy. With Moran's findings we are into the territory Pat Barker later explored in her portrait of Dr W.H.R. Rivers in *Regeneration* (1991) and, of course, we are on the road to a modern understanding of combat stress.

As for his own finite stock of courage, in the trenches of the First World War Moran was awarded the MC during the Battle of the Somme for conspicuous gallantry and devotion to duty and the Italian Silver Medal for Military Valour during a raid. Sometimes he was digging out wounded men at great personal risk, attending to them, and returning again and again to do the same under heavy barrages. So, the abrupt, uncompromising, unclubbable and occasionally dyspeptic fifty-eight year-old, who in Britain's darkest hour of the Second World War was called (on Bracken and Beaverbrook's recommendation) to be Churchill's personal doctor, had wide experience not just of the corridors of power but of the very worst the world could throw at a man.

From 24th May 1940, from his first days of keeping an eye on his famous patient, Moran started to keep a diary, though it was, as I said, forbidden. There were political as well as personal and medical considerations for this prohibition, as the puritanical doctor knew better than anyone. There was the issue of patient privacy and there was the matter of national security. Half the battle for a doctor, Moran claimed, was to know his patient well, so he kept notes.

Detailed notes.

Did the detailed notes became paragraphs?

When does taking detailed notes as a doctor slide into keeping a diary? Keeping a diary was more than bad form. It really was not done. That he did so and continued to take the risks is part of the thrill of reading the book. It is inside track, and he should not be doing it. Where *The Anatomy of Courage* is a measured and sobering and analytical look back at his findings on what was happening to men's minds in the trenches, *Churchill: the Struggle for Survival* feels an exciting, edgy, every day slice of life; and life at the very highest levels. We are on the national stage, or if we are not we are in the wings. Even if we are in the wings we are close. Or we are actually eavesdropping on the humming and hawing. We are on long flights. We are in on late night chats – at Chartwell or at Chequers – or gossiping over lunch. We hear of clashes between leading politicians. Stalin, Roosevelt, Eden, they're all there, as well as Clementine and what she called Churchill's cronies (Beaverbrook and Bracken). Over an unguarded late night glass or two Churchill takes Moran into his confidence. We have a privileged seat, or at least a privileged peep from behind closed doors with a caustically critical observer.

On every page we can see that Moran has a piercing eye for the telling detail and a sharp sense of how to shape an anecdote. The revelations are both private and public. We get to know Churchill as if we are there, at his bedside when the symptoms flare up, or dealing with his regular anxieties, the strain and the stress, or sitting next to him on a long haul plane. Is the old carcass losing his powers? Worse, is the old boy seriously going gaga? After his stroke in 1953, the barely mentioned concern is, should a man in that condition continue as Prime Minister?

On a personal level Moran considered his care for Churchill, his professional diagnosis and his constant encouragement, as his own contribution to the war effort. He saw his job as keeping Churchill on his feet and his daily challenge to get the resolute Churchill over another of his 'hurdles.' For his part, in his war memoirs Churchill called Moran 'a devoted and personal friend to whose unfailing care I probably owe my life.' And Moran's diary – with its great respect for 'this star of England' and his unparalleled willpower – *is* a contribution, however controversial its revelations.

You cannot, of course, avoid the question: does Moran in particular, and do diarists in general, aim to tell the unvarnished truth or do they hope to appear, if ever they are published, as rather more important people than they really were? Do they place themselves right there on stage when in fact they were either in the wings or not even in the theatre? Do they wish to come across as more important than or as important as the world leaders or distinguished diplomats? Do they long to be seen as central players, *confidants*, irreplaceable people? Do they try to appropriate a position in history which they have not earned and did not in reality hold?

Certainly Sir Jock Colville, who was not only Churchill's private secretary but very much in his inner circle, used *The Fringes of Power: Downing Street Diaries 1939-1955* to put the doctor firmly in his place. 'Lord Moran was never present when history was made, though he was quite often invited to luncheon afterwards': a very snobbish and very 'English' put-down which tells you as much about Colville as Moran.

The personal and scholarly feud over Moran's decision to publish his diary rumbled on. In his book *In Search of Churchill*

(1994) Sir Martin Gilbert, Churchill's most distinguished biographer, questioned whether *The Struggle for Survival* can be safely used as a source. At a medical library in London, many years after Moran's death, Martin Gilbert asked to see a diary entry for a single date but was told there was not one for that day although an entry under that exact date appears in Moran's book. Gilbert was further informed that 'it was not a diary in the accepted sense of the word.' He found this position disturbing, and it was 'mind-boggling' for him to think how much misinformation may have crept into history books in this way.

In 2002 and 2006, a new two volume edition was prompted by Lord Moran's son in the hope that he could put an end to this long-running and disparaging debate and, as he saw it, misunderstanding. He maintained that his father's work was not to be seen as a day-by-day record but should be judged on the accuracy of the various notes and notebooks and files his father kept. *Churchill: the Struggle for Survival* was a combination of things scribbled down at the time on the back of envelopes, of some things written soon after the event, as well as considered essays from a later date. It was a 'diary of sorts', an individual picture in constant flux, not an exact chronicle, and unlike other conventional diaries kept by, e.g. Jock Colville.

Diaries can be murky water, in the way that many autobiographies would perhaps find a more honest home if they were placed on the fiction shelves. What are we to make of it if a diarist silently revisits his diary with the benefit of hindsight, putting something in or taking something out or leaving a gap to be later filled? So that, by a re-ordering and re-distributing and re-working, the writer's sharp nose would appear even more infallible than ever? In other words, however it is glossed, in the case of *Churchill: the Struggle for Survival*, did the doctor doctor his own diary? Did he allow himself to put a clear date on entries which he clearly had not written on that date? And, if he did, does that devalue his book, undermine his integrity, suggest he was a bit dodgy, and throw everything else into doubt?

Yes, it is disturbing.

Even so. Even so.

Does it devalue *everything*?

No, not by a long way. I think his instincts as a writer may have taken over – to hell with propriety – and as they did so the old doctor strutted a bit, he overstepped the mark, he was excited, he ironed out discrepancies, he changed a few tenses, he took a few liberties, he gave in to the temptation to pump up his own tyres, as authors who want to be successful and famous sometimes do. Writers, it is routinely claimed, would happily sell their own grandmothers if it led to a few more royalties, but as I sadly never met either of my grandmothers I can't be tested on that one.

What's more, bookish though we may be, don't let's become too unworldly, because the counsel for Moran's defence might well argue that he was spending his days amongst notable politicians and world leaders who themselves were not short on ego, who themselves wanted to stay sitting at the top table longer than they should and even kept their own serious health problems well hidden from the people they represented by persuading the press barons to sit on the story. Moran was surrounded by artful and ambitious men. Over many years he observed those who could not bear the thought of a life without power, men who would cling on to high office at all costs, who kept buggering on year after year by persuading themselves that the world still needed them, who thought that only they could take the heat, orators and strategists and careerists and opportunists who were, not to put too fine a point on it, themselves capable of crossing quite a few lines if it got them what they wanted or where they wanted to be.

Indeed, the defence counsel might suggest that for an example we need look no further than the man who had 'ratted and re-ratted' on his own party, Lord Moran's patient: Winston Churchill.

Diaries, forbidden or otherwise – journals, reliable or otherwise – are a fascinating genre: Evelyn, Pepys, Boswell, Fanny Burney, Darwin and Kafka, companions, critics, observers and commentators. They make you see life differently. They tell you things that no one else knows. And as they employ many of the techniques we are more used to finding in novels we should enjoy them to the full but treat their words with some caution. A diary is not a gospel, and Disraeli only got it half right when he said we converse with the absent by letters and with ourselves by diary. The best diarists write as if for themselves, but *entre nous* in the knowledge that they will be widely read.

The best diarist of the recent past, the freshest, the most intimate, the most alive to every breeze, has been Simon Gray, particularly in his last four memoirs: *The Smoking Diaries* (2004), *The Year of the Jouncer* (2006), *The Last Cigarette* (2008) and *Coda* (2008). I don't think you can write much better or more immediately than the playwright Simon Gray does in his final books. It is a living voice at the height of its power and at the full stretch of its art. It is a voice as individual and unmistakable as Arthur Hugh Clough's. Those Simon Gray diaries – hilarious, entertaining, touching, candid and informative – may well outlive his thirty plays.

As a piece of 'diary' writing, Moran's work may be flawed in principle and somewhat suspect in practice but it is undeniably compelling. It is now over fifty years since *Churchill: the Struggle for Survival* was first published. I bought it straightaway. It felt heavy in my hands, that creamy white hardback with the black and red lettering, with the raised word Churchill repeatedly embossed on the cover. It is sitting on the table next to me in my hut as I write this, and I have just picked it up again. (In fact I ought to add that this is a replacement copy, a first edition originally owned by Malcolm Muggeridge: it has his *Ex Libris* bookplate.)

In 1966 Moran's book drew me in from the first page, and

it has long held me in its grip. Every time I open it I am back there. I am listening again to the voices of the main players of the 1940s and the 1950s: in war and in peace, in the sickroom and in the corridors of power, he was there and I am there, watching from the wings, eavesdropping from the door, or holding the telephone extension when I really shouldn't be.

Reading his doctor's very personal diary sparked my interest in Churchill, bubbling or uncorked or shaky, an interest which has broadened and deepened for full fifty years. Reading Lord Moran's diary also led me to writing two Radio 4 plays, *The Last Bark of the Bulldog*, and *A Portrait of Winston*, one novel, *The Churchill Secret*, and one feature film for television. Reading one book did that.

★

When the treatment takes her close to very personal areas of my body Clare says 'scuse fingers'.

too close for comfort

You asked me, Clare, as people sometimes do after I have given a talk, who is my favourite modern novelist. There are too many to do them justice, too many, but the answer I most often give is:

Brian Moore.

Brian Moore, pronounced *Bree*-an, who started his life in Belfast, Northern Ireland and ended it in Malibu, California, and that journey and all that it implies is perhaps the central thread of his fiction. He wrote twenty novels, nearly all high quality, though those written in his last years were becoming a bit thin. I have read them all, buying most of them in hardback the moment they were published.

Brian Moore was also the favourite novelist of Graham

Greene and you can see why: realistic dialogue, strong and thrilling narratives, Catholic guilt and sin, ambivalence, the moment of moral choice and the drama of the soul. The big difference between the two novelists was that they went in opposite directions, Graham Greene towards Rome and Brian Moore, as fast as his legs would carry him, the other way.

If I mention at random half of Brian Moore's books one or two may ring a bell: *The Lonely Passion of Judith Hearne*, *I am Mary Dunne*, *Black Robe*, *Catholics*, *The Doctor's Wife* – a very erotic novel, this one, one that may have sparked up a number of dull, stale, tired marriage beds – *Cold Heaven*, *The Colour of Blood*, *No Other Life*, *The Statement*, *Lies of Silence*. He also wrote thrillers under a pseudonym. He wrote screenplays, too; for example he was commissioned to write Hitchcock's *Torn Curtain*, which proved to be a dispiriting experience. He was shortlisted for the Booker Prize three times.

Yet go into a bookshop now and try to find even one of Brian Moore's books and you will be lucky. Bree-an Moore? The assistants look blank. He seems unknown. Yes, there is fashion in literature, as in all things, and reputations rise and fall, particularly after a writer's death, we know all that, but this baffles me because he is a writer who rarely puts a foot wrong.

He writes spare, quiet, dispassionate prose – prose that reverberates but does not posture. It stays in the mind. He has a nose for a story, for riveting plots and for conscience-stricken characters. He is interested in lives that are at risk, in people whose safety may be dramatically threatened by violence or those who are in a slow spiral down. A creative chameleon, Moore writes about faith and its loss, church and state, marriage and marital problems, sexual frustration and domestic deceit, revolutionary violence and suburban boredom. He is, in short, a sympathetic virtuoso, an expert who has somehow disappeared off the literary map to be replaced by many who can't write as well and by many who don't have as much to say.

I first came across him in the late 1970s. Philippa Harrison, who published my novels for twenty-five years, asked me if I had read *Catholics* (1972). I had not. I had read nothing of his. Try *Catholics* she said. I'll send it you. You're on his wavelength.

Catholics is set in the Abbey of Muck, on a tiny island off the west coast of Ireland. The brotherhood there is firmly holding to its traditional forms of worship while under heavy pressure from the Vatican to get up to speed. The Abbey is not moving with the times. It refuses to update. By sticking to the old ceremonies of worship it is, however, in danger of becoming a nostalgic talking point and a tourist attraction: in other words, an embarrassment to Rome and the ecumenical movement. The monks on Muck don't want anything to do with 'singing and guitars and turning to touch your neighbour, play-acting and nonsense to make the people come to church the way they used to go to the parish hall for a bingo game.' To add to the drama the Abbot himself is suffering a crisis of faith, a crisis hidden from those he dutifully and loyally leads.

At barely eighty generously printed pages the novel is a marvel of concision. It has perfect lucidity and is deeply affecting.

I then started to read Brian Moore in chronological order. His first two novels were *The Lonely Passion of Judith Hearne* (1955) – about an alcoholic woman for whom life is a letdown – and *The Feast of Lupercal* (1958) – about an ineffectual male schoolteacher for whom life has in some ways never really started. And I want to settle on the second, *The Feast of Lupercal*, partly because my second novel, *The English Lover* (1977) explored similar territory though, as I said, I had read no Brian Moore by that stage.

Both these early Moore novels take place in rainy Belfast, on Moore's overcast home turf, on drab days when frustration and exasperation is the norm. Despite this both are wonderfully accomplished, droll fictions. They have a distinctive Mr Bleaney voice, a voice like Philip Larkin's: a true voice.

Let's step into the confessional, shall we, and face the issue straightaway: for me *The Feast of Lupercal* is too close for comfort. Diarmuid Devine ('Dev') is a thirty-seven year-old English graduate. He teaches at Ardath College, an all boys Catholic school, part boarding, part day pupils. Indeed he had been a boarder there himself. The college is run on traditional lines by a mixture of priests and lay staff, and run with plenty of sarcasm and cane to restore order. As had been the case for centuries in such schools, the birch and the book kept constant company. Even the bell makes its coercive point. Every forty minutes 'an electric bell, deafeningly loud, screamed out in the corridors, crying unheard in empty dormitories, echoing across wet playing fields to die in the faraway mists over Belfast Lough.' That sounds familiar.

The story opens with Dev locked in a cubicle in the masters' lavatory at school, a masterly scene where he overhears two colleagues talking about him. He wonders should he cough or something. One of them calls him 'that old woman' who 'wouldn't know anything about what a fellow feels about girls.' The other colleague chuckles. Dev sits in silence in his cubicle, holding his breath, his face getting hot, and then hotter. He has never been so mortified in his life. Did they mean that he was odd or a pansy?

Flushed and shamefaced, he hurries with a stitch in his side to his next class – *Macbeth*, Act Two, scene one – where he is sharp with his pupils. Seizing the first opportunity to take it out on the boys, he punishes Deegan and McAleer who have not completed their homework. (The novel begins with a caning and reaches its climax with a caning.) The cane whistles down and Deegan doubles over in pain. Then it whistles down on McAleer. Deegan is asked to read the part of Macbeth, 'if he has recovered from his fearful torment'. Later in the lesson, McAleer is handed the role of Lady Macbeth.

Meanwhile Dev sits in the front, fuming. Oh, an old woman

was he! First the sermon, then the punishment. He would not be made a laughing stock.

Back in his bachelor digs he takes his twice-weekly bath. He looks at his white body. He was not ugly but he had never had much luck with girls. He did not have far to look for the reason: it was not his body, his body was not the problem, 'it was the education in Ireland', the priest-ridden education he knew all too well. After all, he'd been a boarder himself, hadn't he, 'shut off from girls until he was almost a grown man. It was a matter of ignorance, pure and simple.' As for thinking about women, he was sure he was perfectly normal.

Though I do not pretend to all the parallels and every detail, *The Feast of Lupercal* took me back to my own schooldays in Wales. It was more or less the same world. It was an all boys' school, a religious foundation with a chapel that dates from the thirteenth century, mostly boarding, some day pupils, and set in a place that had once been a Dominican Priory.

As well as taking me back to my Welsh schooldays – to Classics, to *Macbeth*, chapel, rugby and caning – the Irish novel also took me back to my early years as teacher in an all boys Scottish boarding school – to Classics, to *Macbeth*, chapel, rugby and caning. I had grown up in all this and yet had chosen to stay in the system.

So that covers, Ireland, Wales and Scotland.

Only England left.

And for those of us who have made similar fools of ourselves, who have all too painfully been there, the failed sexual encounter between Dev and Una Clarke in his bachelor digs, with her stealing out in the backyard pallor of dawn, hits the mark. The chapter is a *tour de force*. Every word of it makes me wince.

Did I just then mention a girl? A girl?

Yes, because at a party given by a colleague, Dev falls for Una, the colleague's niece. She is a twenty year-old would-be nurse from Dublin, a Protestant on the rebound from being 'mixed up with a married man.' With Protestants, with people like Una, an affair with a married man was deemed possible. That was the Catholic view because with Protestants 'anything was possible.' Protestant girls were fast. Una is a Protestant girl. Una is a Protestant girl with 'a past'. Hot stuff. Everyone knew that.

And Una liked Dev. She smiled at him. She talked to him. Filled with outrageous joy Dev is drawn into a relationship with Una which develops promisingly. He coaches her for a part in a play, a part which she does not get because 'this city was made up of cliques, drama cliques, religious cliques, school cliques, and God knows what else. There was no use a fellow trying to fight them'. Never mind, he thinks about her all the time. He looks at his reflection in shop windows. He has a right to live. They drink. They go dancing. He is in love. He wants to marry her. They end up, as they must, tiptoeing into his digs:

> Fumbling, as though he were drunk, he pulled off his tie and collar. Shirt over his head. Socks off. It was cold in the moonlit room and as the cold chill of the linoleum touched his toes, another coldness came upon him. He would fail. He did not feel able. Desire was a fantasy, a sinful, secret lusting that ran wild with unfulfilment. Desire was a mental lusting, a making of improbable dreams. But this was no dream: reality was getting ready in the next room. Naked, waiting to be sinned with; waiting to be touched, to be dominated, to be lain on. Oh, let her not come. At least, until he got these things off. Now. Shove them under the bed.

> But now, in the dresser mirror, his long pale body was shamefully exposed. His legs seemed knock-kneed, and his hair was tousled like an idiot's. He backed into the shadows behind the bed. Was that her? Yes, he could hear her coming up the hall. Would she laugh like the girl in the pub last night?

Would she?

'Where are you, Dev?'

Tragically, comically, nothing happens. Or rather everything that matters happens. Both Dev and Una are virgins. They are a couple of innocents. Far from being fast, she does not know what to do, and Dev doesn't want to do it. They get away with it, with doing nothing, and she makes her early morning escape.

Except that, this being Dev and this being Belfast and this being a boys' school, somehow 'the disgrace' gets out. There is graffiti in the boys' urinals, and soon things are out of control. Would the humiliated Dev be sacked? Or would there be a cover-up (to save the school) and it would all be allowed to blow over? Given the scandal, should Una go back to Dublin or, even better, go to England where she could hide her shame, to England where all the Fallen Girls go?

For all its intensely personal setting, the novel ends, as it began, with the same spare, quiet, low-key, dispassionate prose. Dev says he will see her off at the station to say goodbye but he knows he won't:

> Beside him, in the avenue, horse and cart waited idle, as their owner offered wood blocks by the bag at the front door across the way. The horse's head moved like a mine detector along the gutter, reins slack over the strong back. Mr Devine, watching as Una turned the corner, absently put out his hand and fondled the horse's neck. The powerful muscles fluttered at his unexpected touch and the horse swung its head up, looking wildly down the avenue in the narrow focus of its blinkers. Horse and man looked down the avenue, and there was no one there. The horse, harnessed, dumb, lowered its head once more. The man went back into the house.

On one level, of course, Brian Moore is taking his revenge on blinkered Belfast respectability, on the non-life of his own priest-ridden education at St Malachy's College. He is shaking it off, all of it. If you ever can. His later novels, written as a naturalised Canadian, and then as a resident in California, are notable for their secular settings, for their sexual liberation and for the centrality of the female role. Indeed, *I Am Mary Dunne* and *The Temptation of Eileen Hughes* are seen from the woman's point of view. Yes, he returns to Belfast for some of his later novels but to chart terrorist violence in *Lies of Silence* and to explore the explicitly erotic experiences of Sheila Redden in *The Doctor's Wife*.

In a last move, if not a last twist, from this most liberal, effortless and surprising of writers, Brian Moore was buried, as he wished, in Connemara. After the long years of rejection he did come home to Ireland, then, but not to his birthplace, not to the city of Belfast. From Connemara or Kerry he might, I fancy, glimpse the fictional Isle of Muck – there is a real one in Scotland but not in Ireland – where he set *Catholics*, one of his purest novels:

> The fog lifted. The island was there. The visitor walked to the end of the disused pier and saw it across three miles of ocean, riding the sea like an overturned fishing-boat. Morning sunlight moved along a keel of mountain, above valleys as black as tarred boatsides.

I've long thought there is something of Montaigne about Brian Moore, something solitary, deeply sceptical, something in his makeup that I suspect never really settled. Brian Moore entertained doubt. He depended on his own eyes and his own judgement. He never signed up for anything, apart from trying to say it as he saw it. I have always warmed to such people, to people who are not too at one with their community or flock or tribe or religion, and above all I find I am drawn to those who do not know the answers.

I met Brian Moore only once, if you can call a London book signing a meeting. After he had given a reading and been interviewed on stage I stood in a long queue with a small selection of my hardback copies: I was too embarrassed to hold up proceedings by opening my two bulging plastic bags and plonking the full load down in front of him. He signed them and said thank you and gave me a wry smile. He is a writer, and he was in many ways a man, after my own heart. Or so I like to imagine.

★

Jonathan, can't remember if I told you, but I'm going on a three day PD course next weekend, and I'm pretty sure we will improve our understanding and treatment.

I should have asked you first, but I've given the organisers your name as someone who might be willing to write about your condition.

★

Upped my medication today. Didn't want to, I really didn't, but the talk is now about the quality of life left.

Are door-frames getting narrower?

Meanwhile, and it's a long shot, I wonder if I can persuade any new readers to give Anthony Powell a go. But before I do, as a bonus, here's a poem by one of my favourite poets:

One Flesh

Lying apart now, each in a separate bed.
He with a book, keeping the light on late,
She like a girl dreaming of childhood,
All men elsewhere – it is as if they wait
Some new event: the book he holds unread,
Her eyes fixed on the shadows overhead.

Tossed up like flotsam from a former passion,
How cool they lie. They hardly ever touch,
Or if they do it is like a confession
Of having little feeling – or too much.
Chastity faces them, a destination
For which their whole lives were a preparation.

Strangely apart, yet strangely together,
Silence between them like a thread to hold
And not wind in. And time itself's a feather
Touching them gently. Do they know they're old,
These two who are my father and my mother
Whose fire, from which I came, has now grown
　　　cold?

Elizabeth Jennings (1926-2001)

★

Pole – Powell

Far from being drawn to, for a long time I shied away from
the work of Anthony Powell, steering well clear of him more,
I admit, for social rather than literary reasons. He did not seem
a man after my own heart. He – and even more so his world
– struck me as precious, snobbish, self-regarding, entitled and
'Etonian' in the worst way. He sounded an overly-assured
member of a languidly mannered and drawling circle where
any display of enthusiasm would be seen as gauche, one of the
group who smiled wearily at your jokes, a member of that well
bred society in which everyone seemed related to everyone else
and where the game was always to appear underwhelmed and
unimpressed.

It only got worse when I was told that his surname was to be
pronounced 'Pole' not '*Powell*' (as in towel). And when the same
people kept calling him Proustian that put the tin lid on it. I

hadn't read Proust and I hadn't read Pole and I didn't intend to and I was proud of it.

I was wrong.

While I still haven't quite got round to reading Proust's *A la recherche du temps perdu*, I have read Powell's *A Dance to the Music of Time*, all twelve volumes, twice, now on my third time, and I have loved every sentence: twenty-five years of extraordinary fiction, from the opening of *A Question of Upbringing* (1951) to the end of *Hearing Secret Harmonies* (1975). In no time Powell's tone disarmed me. Highly textured and patterned and painterly and detailed though his novels are, I whipped through them at a gathering pace, laughing on the way, marvelling at the skill with which the interlocking stories unfolded, and pausing only to ring up my daughter to go on about …

How good is this bloke Pole, he gets you from the start, his schooldays, there's this small group of Eton friends, Becky, well it's obviously Eton though he doesn't say so, this is just after the First World War, and they play a brilliant trick on their housemaster, and there's a trip to France, then there's university life, Oxford, he nails it, you'll absolutely love that, still rings true, it's so funny, and book after book you keep unexpectedly bumping into people you've met before, you know, as you do in life, you get to know characters who then go missing and sink only to resurface, and themes go underground in much the same way, it's full of coincidences, London parties and drink and country houses, debs and tarts, *beau monde* and *demi-monde*, quite a bit on the army, not surprising as Pole-Powell was from an army family, but it's mainly artists and cranks and eccentrics and writers and aimless wasters, tarnished silver spoons, a wonderfully varied world in all kinds of hot water, power-conscious politicians, publishing, scriptwriting, journalism, reviewing, (Powell edited *Punch*), a cast of grotesques, bohemians, feckless aristos, hangers-on, middle class pushies, there's a bit too much on the occult for my taste, a section in Wales, he has Welsh blood so that's another bonus, lots of affairs, strange couplings, hopeless marriages and complex competitive love lives, then it's the Second World War, in fact he covers most things from the early 1920s to the late '60s, that's half the twentieth century dammit, right up to hippies and Flower Power, I don't know how he does it but he does and it gets you, honestly, it gets to the inner truth, and it's only just over a million words long …

So my daughter Becky joined in the race, snatching each volume of the twelve out of my hand. I'm not sure who read the cycle in the shorter time. It was a close run thing.

Two things in particular interest me as a reader and as a writer: the way Anthony Powell handles his narrative, and the way his humour works.

Both are difficult to pin down.

As narrator and anchorman, Nick Jenkins is an introvert and clearly modelled on Powell's own life: an only child of army parents, the novelist and the narrator-novelist have much in common. Nick Jenkins is not a strong presence. He comes over as slightly cold-blooded and slightly bemused, yet that is part of the subtle charm and the elusive magic of the sequence. You suspect he fell into being a novelist rather than chose it. Time passes and disposes of us all, and as you read on he feels to be both there and not there, central and marginal. For considerable sections of the cycle you are not fully aware of him. He gets married and he has children – such massive elements of a life – but all that doesn't seem to register strongly: it's almost by-the-by. ('To think at all objectively about one's own marriage is impossible.' In the war he concedes 'Like a million others, I missed my wife.')

There is a kind of intimacy and a kind of detachment, a kind of aesthetic distancing. He's diffident and resigned but not exactly retiring, more a watcher than a doer, not naïve exactly but slow to pick up the way that things are going on around him: somewhat adrift, remiss, clicking in and out of tune, drifting in and out of focus, as I often feel I have been (and still am) in my own life but for many years did not wish to acknowledge or admit.

As Robert Burton (one of Anthony Powell's favourites) puts it in *The Anatomy of Melancholy* (1621), writing flows rather as a river:

> A River runs sometimes precipitate and swift, then dull and slow; now direct, then winding; now deep, then shallow, now muddy, then clear; now broad, then narrow, doth my style flow; now serious, then light; now comical, then satirical; now more elaborate, then remiss, as the present subject required, or as the time I was affected.

One of the first decisions, and one of the biggest, you make as a novelist is whether to write the book in the third person or the first. What is the centre of the consciousness? The intensely personal first person is instantly appealing, especially if you are in confessional mode, but as time passes it can run out on you. One set of eyes and one set of ears can become more a limitation than a freedom. I once sent a first person novel to my publisher only to contact her the very next day saying send it back, don't be silly she said, you're in no state to judge, I mean it I said, don't read it. Three months later I submitted the story retold in the third person.

'Reading novels,' as X Trapnel, another novelist, says in *Temporary Kings*, 'needs almost as much talent as writing them.' And *A Dance to the Music of Time* is a kind of master class in writing fiction. It is in the first person but feels more third. As well as anchoring the story, Nick Jenkins, novelist-scriptwriter-general observer, reflects on the structure and architecture of fiction, on objectivity and subjectivity, the way facts work (or don't) in novels, and on the importance of understatement yet the attendant risk that understatement can lead to evasion.

What is the source of imagination? Is fiction superior to biography? Do you learn more about the writer by reading his fiction than by reading his confessions? Add in the thorny question of realism/naturalism, how to overcome your fear of critics and how to deal with publishers, ('It's always a temptation for a publisher to have a go at writing a book. After all, they think, if authors can do that, anyone can.') and you have a sense of how Powell works.

His humour is as difficult to pin down, or is especially difficult to demonstrate by quotation. With Evelyn Waugh and Kingsley Amis and E.M. Forster, selecting a representatively funny passage would be easy. But with Powell there are long and brilliant set pieces in which one is smiling or laughing or dazzled by the sustained skill. It's more a question of overall tone. It's like having a witty, droll, sharply observant friend – who sees comic potential in everything – whispering wickedly in your ear. There is farce. There are grotesque moments. He can be sardonic, hilarious, absurdly funny, grimly funny, darkly funny, and he mingles all these rather as Shakespeare does.

Here are three examples where he is being droll, sharp, reflective, but to feel their power you have to be fully involved in the novels, to be caught up in the world:

> I was impressed for the ten thousandth time by the fact that literature illuminates life only for those to whom books are a necessity. Books are unconvertible assets, to be passed on only to those who possess them already.

> He suddenly began to look wretched, much as I had seen him look as a schoolboy: lonely: awkward: unpopular: odd; no longer the self-confident businessman into which he had grown. His face now brought back the days when one used to watch him

plodding off through the drizzle to undertake the long, solitary runs across the dismal fields beyond the sewage farms: runs which were to train him for teams in which he was never included.

For reasons not always at the time explicable, there are specific occasions when events begin suddenly to take on a significance previously unsuspected, so that, before we really know where we are, life seems to have begun in earnest at last, and we ourselves, scarcely aware that any change has taken place, are careering uncontrollably down the slippery avenues of eternity.

Though he writes beautifully timed and beautifully shaped sentences, his modulated tone and perfect ear works best when developed in longer sweeps, like a theme in a symphony, and I would ask you to read him and see if it strikes you so.

And of course the central portrait of Kenneth Widmerpool, that ludicrous, sinister, dangerous, disturbing, and deadly serious man – first seen on a solitary training run at school and last glimpsed on a jog in the mist before collapsing in the road – is a comic creation of genius.

★

on re-reading

When embarrassed by how patchily read I am, and especially so when being pressed by my family or friends, I often claim to be re-reading the book in question, trotting out because 'it's so many years now since I first came across it'. In fact my memory is neither the issue nor the excuse. The plain truth is that I often haven't got a clue about the book in question because I have never opened it.

There are some books, however, that I have read and re-read, many more books than Anthony Powell's, and I am not finished with any of them yet. The first thing that caught my eye on recently re-opening *Silas Marner* was the epigraph from Wordsworth.

> A child, more than all other gifts
> That earth can offer to declining man,
> Brings hope with it, and forward-looking
> > thoughts.

The words not only caught my eye but held it. Old age, declining years, the gift of a child ... how apt a quotation to place at the beginning of the tale of Silas and Eppie. But before I could even start to reread the novel, my mind was side-tracked from prose to poetry, from George Eliot to Wordsworth.

At first I could not precisely place the lines of poetry, and this annoyed me. After all, Wordsworth is a favourite writer. I should know this stuff. But it's an age since I last taught his poem 'Michael' in the classroom. Over the years I think I rather lost confidence in teaching Wordsworth and felt – so much did he mean to me – unwilling to fight the good fight for modest plain lives, for simple childhoods, for old-fashioned stories in rural settings. I had lost the habit, and the *Lyrical Ballads* disappeared from my desk.

I got my Collected Wordsworth, Oxford Standard Authors edition, down from the shelves and lightly banged off the dust. 'Michael', written in 1800, is four hundred and eighty lines long and I was immediately drawn back and up into the mountains. Set in a special place in the Lake District, not far from Grasmere, it is subtitled 'A pastoral poem'. I first read both it and George Eliot's rural tale at the same stage of my life. In the late 1950s I was a schoolboy in Wales, just another muddled and preoccupied teenager. It was a time when I was also beginning to escape, sometimes (like Dylan Thomas, as you may remember) striding along from Swansea to the Gower coast, but usually inland on the Brecon Beacons, walking the long ridges, sometimes with friends but more often than not alone.

In the foothills of the Beacons I stepped over streams and skirted isolated farmyards and was barked at by sheepdogs. I passed places very like the shepherd Michael's cottage. On higher ground, I occasionally noticed obscure mounds of stones, places which felt special if not sacred, and uncannily close in spirit to Wordsworth's Lake District.

And, as so often when reading Wordsworth, it is the precise sense of place (take the A591 out of Grasmere) which strikes you.

> If from the public way you turn your steps
> Up the tumultuous brook of Green-head Ghyll
> You will suppose that with an upright path
> Your feet must struggle; in such bold ascent
> The pastoral mountains front you, face to face,
> But courage!

Wordsworth is walking with us, guiding our steps to the forest side in Grasmere Vale where dwelt Michael, a shepherd.

> Nor should I have made mention of this Dell,
> But for one object which you might pass by,
> Might see and notice not. Beside the brook
> Appears a straggling heap of unhewn stones!
> And to that simple object appertains
> A story ...

And that begins Wordsworth's story, a story with more than a hint of the Prodigal Son. The strong old shepherd Michael has a younger wife, 'a woman of a stirring life'. They are hard-working, thrifty people and the light of their lives is their only child, their son Luke. In him they invest their love, and the bonds between the three of them feel unbreakably strong.

Unravelling the threads and parallels and contrasts between the poem and George Eliot's novel feels right because hard-working weavers are at the heart of the matter: Isabel, Michael's wife, a comely matron twenty years younger, is (like Silas Marner) a weaver:

> Whose heart was in her house: two wheels she
>   had
> Of antique form; this large, for spinning wool;
> This small, for flax; and, one wheel had rest,
> It was because the other was at work ...

Isabel and Michael are 'a proverb in the vale for their endless industry', and after supper, by the light of the old lamp, Luke often lends his mother a hand at the fireside loom.

A tale which promises a happy ending for four hundred and forty lines is, however, brought to a brutally shocking conclusion when Luke, at eighteen, goes off the rails. It is heavy news. After all the years of quiet and deep parental care, after ten pages of poetry, comes the car crash. The family's sad fate takes Wordsworth only six plain, unsparing lines:

> Meantime Luke began
> To slacken in his duty; and, at length,
> He in the dissolute city gave himself
> To evil courses: ignominy and shame
> Fell on him, so that he was driven at last
> To seek a hiding-place beyond the seas.

How different an ending it is for Silas.

Silas Marner, published sixty years after 'Michael', is George Eliot's most strongly poetic novel. It can be seen as her own lyrical ballad, a reading her epigraph from Wordsworth surely invites.

As well as walking the Welsh hills in the 1950s, I was beginning to read George Eliot in a serious way. I started with *The Mill on the Floss*, and then, as a set book for A Level, I moved on to *Middlemarch*, which remains an unmatched experience, but it is the fate of the wronged Weaver of Raveloe that pulls most at me: her third novel stays so clearly woven and interwoven into my memory. As I re-read it, George Eliot invites me to sit at Silas's spinning wheel, to live his solitary days in solitary ways, to be a man with no wife and no child, to feel what it is to be a disinherited remnant, and to embrace the isolated, the unknown and the unlike.

I have never, as I said, been able to shake off the story of that stranger, Silas Marner, that pallid, short-sighted, mysterious, under-sized man who (earlier in his life) has been falsely accused of theft and cast out by a narrow religious sect.

Short though it is, the novel opens out into the loving story of Silas and Eppie, the golden-haired child, as well as the story of the Cass brothers, the fate of Molly and of Nancy Lammeter, indeed into a portrait of the whole close-knit Raveloe community from squire to pub. It is on a much smaller scale than *Middlemarch*, of course, but as short and as fine as *Middlemarch* is fine and long. Indeed, we know from her letters that George Eliot initially considered writing *Silas Marner* as a poem. Is it, in a sense, her response to 'Michael'?

Wordsworth's old shepherd is left alone with a pile of stones, sitting with his faithful dog by the sheepfold that he and Luke would never finish building. He is an object of pity. With the Weaver of Raveloe the opposite is the case: Silas is protected by love, and chosen by his 'daughter' Eppie, who rejects the offer of a comfortable materialistic life with her natural father, Godfrey Cass. Their garden was 'fenced with stones on two sides, but in front there was an open fence, through which the flowers shone with answering gladness ... "O father," said Eppie, "what a pretty home ours is! I think nobody could be happier than we are.'"

Things turn out well for Silas, then, as he deserves. In time he is integrated into the community as Raveloe comes to accept him, even to embrace him.

Sentimental? Is it sentimental to picture a drug-addicted mother dying in the snow while her child crawls to safety and a life of warm support? Is it a sentimental thing to believe that love has more meaning and more value than coins, however brightly they shine in your hands and however high the heap under your floorboards?

★

marks upon the snow

> From our low seat beside the fire
>   Where we have dozed and dreamed and watched
> the glow
>   Or raked the ashes, stopping so
> We scarcely saw the sun or rain
>   Above, or looked much higher
> Than this same quiet red or burned-out fire.
>   Tonight we heard a call.
>   A rattle on the window-pane,
>   A voice on the sharp air,
> And felt a breath stirring our hair,
>   A flame within us: something swift and tall
>   Swept in and out and that was all.
> Was it a bright or dark angel? Who can know?
>   It left no mark upon the snow,
>   But suddenly it snapped the chain
>   Unbarred, flung wide the door
>   Which will not shut again;
> And so we cannot sit here any more.

We must arise and go.
The world is cold without
And dark and hedged about
With mystery and enmity and doubt,
But we must go
Though yet we do not know
Who called, or what marks we shall leave upon
the snow.

Charlotte Mew (1869-1928)

★

As I've said before, and I'll say it again, Clare, you got me singing, so much so I can hear Leonard Cohen's unmistakable voice as I tap out these words. You got me singing when I thought I couldn't carry on, when I thought my last book would be my last word, when I'd all but thrown in the towel. Encouraged by your care and loosened by your touch, you got me singing in a freewheeling way, singing the only song I ever had, except now there are two of us on a tandem, meeting up on the road with a cross dressing actor, an idealistic communist, a one-legged poet, a two-legged poet, a short story writer, a weaver, a shepherd, a doctor, a Scot, a Welshman, an Irishman, a gay novelist, an Etonian novelist, an American playwright and a Nazi. Not bad company, not a bad haul from a bit of freewheeling on your bike. And all this took me back to Shakespeare and George Eliot and Wordsworth, the loves of my life, and, by chance, back to Wales.

I studied *King Lear* as a boy, you may remember, in the late 1950s, and again as an undergraduate in the early 1960s. And as I said near the outset of this book, I then edited the play in my mid twenties, wrestling with Quartos, Folios, with scholarly emendations, various readings and sources, not to mention writing line by line explanatory notes, by the end of which three year stint I nearly knew the whole thing off by heart – and I was of course shaken to my core. Because, at whatever age you are, young girl or old man, *King Lear* is a work that you can never forget. It knocks you sideways.

And over the years I taught the play on countless occasions in my classroom, with the roles often memorably read by generations of pupils. I also saw it performed on stage or screen by Paul Scofield, Michael Hordern, Michael Gambon, Derek Jacobi, Robert Stephens, Timothy West and Anthony Hopkins: Lear the enraged, Lear the blind, the tyrant, the self-pitying, the noble, the unbearable, the masterful, the violent, the mad, the deluded, the soulful, the redeemed: Lear was part or some or all of these.

As for me, I am now myself, like the king, a foolish, fond old man, four score and upward, but whether or not I am in my perfect mind, I leave to others.

–Right, Jonathan. On the plinth. On your back, please. Take your time.

ACKNOWLEDGEMENTS

My thanks to Gail Pirkis at *Slightly Foxed* and to Nicola Beauman at Persephone.

I am most grateful to Robert Hyde, my excellent editor and Galileo Publishers.

And to Gillie, these simple words: thank you for our lifetime together.